Teachers' Resource Book

Story-writing
SCAFFOLDS

Written by
Julie Allaway and Maria Roberts

HOPSCOTCH

A division of MA Education Ltd

Published by Hopscotch
A division of MA Education Ltd
St Jude's Church
Dulwich Road
Herne Hill
London SE24 0PB

Tel: 020 7738 5454

© 2008 MA Education Ltd

Written by Julie Allaway and Maria Roberts
Series design by Blade Communications
Cover illustration by Kirsty Wilson
Illustrated by Jane Bottomley
Printed in the UK by CLE

ISBN 978-1-90430-725-9

Julie Allaway and Maria Roberts hereby assert their
moral right to be identified as the author of this work
in accordance with the Copyright, Designs and
Patents Act, 1988.

Story-writing SCAFFOLDS

CONTENTS

INTRODUCTION

Story-writing Scaffolds for Year 4 is intended for use in schools to help teach children how to write effective short stories in a variety of different genres. It improves children's ability to organise their writing so that it has purpose by familiarising them with a system of planning stories which they can apply to any title. As they work through the units, the children assemble a portfolio of stories containing genre-specific vocabulary and writing features. The chosen text types correspond with those in the Framework's text-level objectives for each half-term.

Each unit also includes information and activities on at least one sentence-level objective. Thus the book also enhances the children's knowledge of grammar, their punctuation and style.

THE PROGRAMME CONTAINS:

a teachers' book comprising:

▨ notes for teachers on the genres
▨ copies of exemplar stories together with teaching notes
▨ guidance on how to develop grammar skills in children's writing
▨ guidance on how to help children write in the particular genre

a resource book of photocopiable material comprising:

▨ illustrated versions of the exemplar stories especially produced for children
▨ notes for the children on understanding the grammar (optional reference material)
▨ photocopiable activity sheets to reinforce the grammar (optional)
▨ notes and tips for the children on writing stories (optional reference material)
▨ differentiated story scaffolds which enable them to choose the course of the story they are about to write
▨ vocabulary banks for them to use and add to.

HOW TO USE THE PROGRAMME

1. After examining examples of stories in the target genre by established writers, read and discuss the exemplar story with the children, using the notes in the margin to highlight the examples of the unit's grammatical teaching point and writing feature. The children should follow the story using their own illustrated version from the Resource book.

2. Next read through and explain the 'Understanding the grammar and punctuation' section of the unit. The children can do the activities orally together or independently on paper.

3. Then explain the 'Helpful hints' and 'Writing features' sections of the unit to the children.

4. Read through the story scaffolds with the children. Then give them the differentiated word banks and ask them to record their own vocabulary suggestions in the space provided.

Give the children time to plan, write and edit their stories. Each child can then store the best copies of their stories in a writing folder.

NOTES FROM THE AUTHORS

The activities in each unit, from reading the model story to composing a story using the scaffolds, can be used in shared or guided time, with the children working collaboratively or individually.

The order of activities for each unit corresponds exactly with the sequence for the teaching of writing outlined in *Grammar for Writing* (DfEE 0107/2000). First the model story can be discussed and its grammatical and thematic features interrogated during shared reading. Next the grammar and punctuation activities can be undertaken to reinforce the children's understanding of the relevant sentence-level objectives. The helpful hints section, story scaffolds and vocabulary banks support the teacher and children in shared writing sessions and in subsequent guided and independent writing.

The method works well with children of all abilities and with bilingual pupils, as it offers the security of a detailed framework and a bank of appropriate vocabulary together with the challenge of a grammar and writing features component for each unit. As the grammar section contains examples from the story, all the children can access it at some level: it is not always necessary to understand the mechanics of the grammar in order to modify the examples for use in an individual story.

The units fulfil the text-level and sentence-level requirements of the NLS Framework for Year 4 and revise components from Year 3. The units may be used specifically in literacy lessons or they may be linked with work in other curriculum areas and used accordingly.

TERM 1
UNIT 1
Genre: historical stories
Grammar: verbs, verb tenses, powerful verbs (S2; S3)
Punctuation: commas (S5)
Writing feature: story settings; how the passage of time is presented (T1; T3)

UNIT 2
Genre: adventure stories
Grammar: adverbs (S4)
Punctuation: paragraphs (T15)
Writing features: narrative order (T4)

UNIT 3
Genre: playscripts
Grammar: sentences (S?)
Punctuation: revision of capitals, full stops, question marks, exclamation marks (from Year 3)
Writing features: conventions of playscripts (T13)

TERM 2
UNIT 4
Genre: family stories
Grammar: revision of types of sentences – statement, question, exclamation
Punctuation: revision of speech punctuation
Writing features: collaborative writing and using plans; stories in chapters (T12)

UNIT 5
Genre: fantasy stories
Grammar: adjectives (S1)
Punctuation: contraction; apostrophe (S2)
Writing: expressive and descriptive language (T10; T13)

UNIT 6
Genre: science fiction
Grammar: word order (S3)
Punctuation: possession; apostrophe (S2)
Writing features: develop the use of story settings (T10)

UNIT 7
Genre: horror stories
Grammar: adverbs (S1)
Punctuation: how commas join and separate clauses (S4)
Writing features: creating a sense of fear and uncertainty

TERM 3
UNIT 8
Genre: stories that raise issues
Grammar: plurals (S1)
Punctuation: commas in adverbial phrases and clauses (S4)
Writing features: how issues affect characters (T11)

UNIT 9
Genre: story from another culture – Bahamian story
Grammar: sentence construction (S2; S3)
Punctuation: speech marks (S2)
Writing features: features of Bahamian stories (T2)

UNIT 10
Genre: story from another culture – Maori legend
Grammar: connectives (S4)
Punctuation: colons and semi-colons; parenthetic commas, dashes and brackets (S2)
Writing features: features of Maori stories (T2)

Longboat stowaways

The shadows from the flickering flames played across the weathered lines of the old skald's face; his voice stole into every corner of the longhouse and mesmerised the listeners as they picked at the left-overs from the banquet scattered across the wooden table. In this Viking settlement of Oseberg, Norway, the storytelling was the highlight of Jolablot, the midwinter feast. Tales of the god Odin and his wars against the Frost Giants of Utgard; the rainbow bridge, Bifrost, that stretched from earthly Midgard to the home of the gods at Asgard; these were the characters and places that made up the very fabric of Viking life over a thousand years ago.

Gunneva, the chieftain's daughter was startled from her poetic trance by the cold, clammy nose of her dog, demanding its share of the feast. As she secretly flicked a morsel from a wooden platter, the dull glint of gold winked at her from the rush strewn floor. In the time that she took to pat her dog, the find was secreted in the woad folds of her tunic.

Later, by the dim light of the glowing hearth, she studied her new-found treasure. The lucky charm – the hammer of Thor – lay heavily in her palm. She knew to whom it belonged – her father. She felt sure that he wouldn't miss it; he was a great warrior and trader who had

returned from trips to Miklagard bearing silver, silks and exotic spices. He would never miss this small trinket! A sudden snoring from the sleeping platform made her start guiltily and she tied the charm around her neck with a piece of thread and burrowed into her bed of furs.

At last, winter slowly gave way to spring and, as the days lengthened, preparations were underway for the first of the overseas raids. The settlement was expanding and her father had decided that more slaves were needed to work in the fields. Gunneva was accustomed to slaves doing the really heavy and dirty work around the farm and she had never really given much thought to where they had come from.

One day Gunneva, bored with her task of spinning, ran off to find her best friend Eirik. He was practising his fighting moves with his scramasax and she watched him for a while as he thrust and parried with the single-edged knife.

'Come and see the longboat with me,' begged Gunneva. 'It is almost ready to sail!'

''Willingly!'gasped the exhausted Eirik. 'This shield is so heavy.'

Together the children ran to the beach where the longboat was moored. It was a mighty wooden planked vessel with huge sails and hefty oars, enabling it to quickly overpower smaller boats or escape swiftly from danger. Neither of them had ever been allowed to go aboard.

Excited by the bustle of loading supplies and weapons, Gunneva felt that she wanted to be part of the adventure.

'Let's have a closer look,' she urged. 'Bring your weapons so that we look as if we are helping.'

Everybody was so engrossed in their particular tasks that they did not notice the children scuttling up the gangplank. They hid themselves behind some sacks and watched the proceedings with interest.

'Hey! What have you got there?' suddenly demanded Eirik.

Gunneva realised that the golden charm around her neck had slipped into view.

'It's just something I found and now it belongs to me!' she replied guiltily.

'That's your father's lucky charm. I heard him talking about it the other day with some of the men. He said that he was feeling uneasy about this voyage and wished that he had Thor's hammer to protect them. You need to return it to him before he sails.'

'My father would never be scared! He is a great warrior. He will never sail to Niflheim in a boat of toenail clippings!'

'True, but still you ought to give back what you found.'

Gunneva knew that Eirik was right but she was feeling rebellious. She grabbed at a pottery jar.

'Here, I'm thirsty. Let us have a drink from this and then I will take the charm back to my father.'

The golden liquid was mead, the sweet tasting honey drink, and the children greedily swallowed it down. Soon they were giggling and lightheaded and had to hide themselves under a pile of furs so that they would not be detected. The mead, combined with the warmth of the welcome spring sunshine and the gentle rocking motion of the boat, lulled the youngsters to sleep.

Hours later they awoke. Even with their befuddled brains, they could tell by the rolling and pitching that the longboat had put to sea. Eirik pushed away the furs and a shower of sea spray hit their faces. The sail was filled with the wind and the mast and ropes creaked and groaned under the strain. The warriors were either tending the ship or sitting around in groups sharpening their battle axes and longswords. Gunneva and Eirik looked at each other in horror – they were going to be in so much trouble!

'Let's just stay hidden for the moment,' whispered Gunneva, diving back under the furs.

The stowaways lost track of the time but their limbs grew stiff and their bellies empty. In the meantime, the boat sailed on around the coast.

Suddenly the noises on the boat changed. The men were rowing hard for the shore and as the boat travelled right onto the beach, the chieftain and his men launched a surprise attack on a coastal monastery. Crouching in the boat, Gunneva and Eirik watched as the warriors forced their way in and captured the monks and the surrounding villagers. There was a lot of screaming and shouting and the clash of weapons as the villagers attempted to repel the invaders. Gunneva saw her father wielding his mighty axe and encouraging his men.

All at once the children heard a thud, then another and another, followed by a strange crackling sound. Burning arrows were being shot into the supplies on the boat and the fire was spreading. The chief glanced back to see what was happening to the longboat and in that instant he was hit by a spear. The remaining warriors on the boat ran to form a defensive wall with their wooden shields so that they could protect their leader. The children were alone on the vessel.

'Quick, we have to save the boat!' shouted Gunneva and without a moment to lose they jumped up and began to beat out the flames.

Choking on the smoke and with their hair singed the children were so engrossed with fighting the flames that they did not realise that the battle was over. The Vikings had been victorious. The monastery had been looted, the fittest folk captured for slaves and foodstores and animals rounded up. There had been casualties on both sides and Gunneva looked around anxiously for her father. He was carried onto the longboat covered in blood from his wound and looking pale and drawn. The other men watched in silence as the two children walked nervously towards him. Gunneva was in tears as she handed the golden charm to the wounded chieftain.

'I have brought back Thor's hammer to you,' she stammered. 'I should never have kept it. I'm sorry.'

Scowling, her father placed the hammer around his neck and then unexpectedly he burst out laughing.

'Trust a daughter of mine to have so much courage! The luck of Thor was with us all when you saved the longboat. Now let us return to Oseberg and send our brave dead on their fiery way to the feasting halls of Valhalla. Odin and Thor both smile on the deeds of men today! You my daughter, I leave to the wrath of your mother!'

Understanding the grammar and punctuation

Verb tenses

A verb is an action word.

The tense of the verb tells us when something is happening.

Here are the different tenses of the verb 'see'.

I saw, I have seen (past)
(something has already happened)

I see, I am seeing, I do see (present)
(something is happening now)

I will see, I will be seeing (future)
(something that will or may happen)

Commas

Commas are used to separate parts of a sentence. They tell the reader when to pause in their reading.

'Quick, we have to save the boat!'

They separate items in a list.
The Viking warriors carried spears, daggers, axes and shields.

They are used to separate any extra information within the sentence.
Gunneva, the chieftain's daughter, was startled from her poetic trance.

Powerful verbs

Powerful verbs give extra meaning to your writing.

They make your writing more exciting.

'Willingly!' <u>said</u> the exhausted Eirik.
'Willingly!' <u>gasped</u> the exhausted Eirik.

The villagers <u>tried to hold off</u> the invaders.
The villagers <u>attempted to repel</u> the invaders.

You can use a thesaurus to find examples of powerful verbs.

Name

Verb tenses

Change the underlined verbs in each of these sentences to the tense in the brackets. Rewrite each sentence

1. The boat _sailed_ on around the coast. (present)

   _____

2. The children _were_ alone on the vessel. (future)

   _____

3. The stowaways _lost_ track of time. (present)

   _____

4. Odin and Thor both _smile_ on the deeds of men today. (past)

   _____

Powerful verbs

Read the following passage. Circle the powerful verbs.

> Crouching in the boat, Gunneva and Eirik watched as the warriors forced their way in and then captured the monks and the surrounding villagers. There was a lot of screaming and shouting and the clash of weapons as the villagers attempted to repel the invaders. Gunneva saw her father wielding his mighty axe and encouraging his men.

Find some powerful verbs to replace the ones in the boxes below.

said	walk	look	go

Commas

Read the following passage. Add commas to punctuate the lists.

We can discover a lot about Viking life from archaeological evidence. Viking farmers grew oats barley wheat and rye as well as vegetables like onions beans and cabbages. They also kept animals such as cows pigs sheep pigs ducks and hens. There was always a lot of work to do. Water had to be fetched from the stream for cooking drinking and washing. Wood for the fire had to be collected chopped stacked and dried ready for use. No wonder the richer Vikings wanted slaves to do the work for them!

Pretend that you are a Viking chieftain getting ready for a raid. Make a list of all the things that you need to take with you on the longboat. Use commas to punctuate your list.

_____

_____

_____

Choose a clause from each of the three columns below to make four complete sentences. Write out the sentences, remembering to add in the commas.

Gunneva	the slave	threw the axe
Thor	the chieftain's daughter	found a lucky charm
Eiri	the thunder god	lived in a monastery
Leif	the monk	sailed in the longboat

1. _____

2. _____

3. _____

4. _____

Now make up three sentences of your own using commas to separate extra information in the sentence.

Helpful hints for writing an historical story

✦ Mention the time when the events of the story take place early on in your story so that the reader understands the historical setting right from the beginning.

✦ When you describe the settings of your story, include details of landscape, buildings and objects that are typical of the historical period in which your story takes place. Weave them into the plot. You are not writing an information text but giving an account of life in the past.

✦ Use a third person narrator to tell your story. Otherwise, if you choose a first person narrator, you will have to use old-fashioned language throughout.

✦ Give your characters names that are suitable for the period in history that the story takes place.

✦ Give the male and female characters in your story roles that are appropriate for the period in history when your story is set.

For example, it would be the Viking men who went on the trading expeditions while the women remained at home. The son would follow the father's trade and the daughter would help her mother in the house.

✦ A good way of showing that your characters are very much 'of their time' is to give them beliefs that were commonly held at the time in which they lived but have since proved to be false. For example, Viking warriors believed that if they died in bed they would be taken to a place in the depths of the Earth in a boat made from toe-nail clippings.

✦ Include historical words and sayings in the dialogue between your characters, but make sure that the expressions you use would have been used in the period you are describing. Use your characters' discussions to give historical information to the reader.

✦ In most historical stories, key figures of the time are mentioned in passing but do not play a central role in the story.

✦ In many cases, the plot of an historical story is already known. Your challenge is to bring events to life by describing the emotions of the characters through their speech, actions and description.

✦ Be careful to avoid historically inaccurate details. For example, it would be wrong to say that Gunneva had buttons or zips on her clothes. Viking garments were fastened with brooches.

Historical story
Scaffold 1

You are going to write an historical story.
To help plan your story, use the framework below.
Choose one option from each stage.

Stage One

Choose the characters for your story.

a) An orphan, whose parents were killed by Viking raiders.
He/she now lives in a monastery under the care of the monks.

b) A child whose father was taken as a slave by Viking raiders.
He/she has to care for the rest of the family.

Stage Two

Start your story with a good beginning.

a) Legs trembling with exertion, the child (make up a suitable name)
clambered back to the top of the cliff, the seagull eggs carefully
stowed in a bag on his/her back. It was then that the tiny sail
on the horizon caught his/her attention – a Viking longboat!

b) The red speck on the horizon was getting closer – it was a
boat! This was the moment they had been dreading – the
Viking raiders had returned.

Stage Three

Set the scene for the story.

The child (name) ran as fast as he/she could to sound the
warning.

a) Everybody thought he/she was playing a joke and told the
child (name) to get on with his/her chores.

b) The news caused chaos as people panicked and tried to flee.

Stage Four

Give the characters a problem.

The wind had died down and the invaders were having to row the Viking boat towards the beach. The child (name) rang the bell which is the signal for trouble.

a) The people decided to stand and fight. Anyone who could handle a weapon waited on the beach for the Viking attack.

b) When they heard the signal, the people took their animals and their precious goods and hid in the secret caves in the cliffs.

Stage Five

Say how the problem is solved.

The Vikings did not know that there were rocks close to the beach. They ran the boat aground and holed it.

a) Most of the Viking warriors were unable to swim and they drowned. Any survivors that made it to the shore were captured and taken prisoner.

b) The Viking warriors realised that they had no means of escape. They swam to shore and fought because they wanted to die honourably in battle.

Stage Six

Say how the story ends.

The battle was won. The people returned to their homes to give thanks and celebrate.

HOW SHALL I END THE STORY?

a) The child (name) was hailed as a hero/heroine and was given a gold cross as a reward.

b) From then on there was always someone on look-out duty to give warnings of any unwelcome visitors.

Historical story
Vocabulary bank 1

alarm	helmet	settlement
ashore	hero	shield
attack	heroine	slavery
	hide	slaves
battle		surrounded
beach	livestock	survivor
brave	longboat	sword
bravery	loot	
		treasure
captives	monastery	trick
cove	monk	
		victorious
dramatic	oars	victory
dwellings		Viking raider
	people	
escape	prisoners	war
		warning
fight	raid	warrior
	row	

My own words

Historical story
Scaffold 2

You are going to write an historical story.
To help plan your story, use the framework below.
Choose one option from each stage.

Stage One

Choose the characters for your story.

In a remote Viking village close to a dense forest there lived:

a) A chieftain's son, who had been sent to live with a foster family so that he could learn how to become a rune-master. He had his own personal slave who was his constant companion.

b) A young man who was an apprentice to a great wood carver. He was learning how to carve the intricate designs that decorated the wooden pillars of the most important Viking buildings.

Stage Two

Start your story with a good beginning.

a) The sky was heavy with snow and the wind wailed eerily through the trees. Ignoring the pleas of the slave to stay within the boundaries of the village, the young man (name) headed into the wilderness.

b) The forest seemed to be full of voices and shadows. The young man (name) shivered as he pulled his cloak around himself. He did not notice a slave who was following him.

Stage Three

Set the scene for the story.

The young man (name) had been given a difficult task. He had to create a wonderful carving (either stone or wood) to prove that he had the skills of a true craftsman. It was his final test.

a) His mind was empty of ideas. He was afraid that he would fail and be sent home in disgrace. He did not notice the softly falling snow all around him.

b) He was so busy thinking about how good he was that he lost his way in the forest.

Stage Four

Give the characters a problem.

The slave was worried because the snow was covering the young man's footprints. Even with snow shoes it was hard to make progress. Hungry wolves caught the humans' scent and trailed them.

a) The young apprentice fell and injured his leg. His cries enabled the slave to find him but he was too heavy to carry through the deep snow.

b) Suddenly the slave broke through the thin ice on a hidden pool. The young man followed his shouts and managed to pull him from the icy water.

The wolves closed in on the helpless men who cried to the gods for help.

Stage Five

Say how the problem is solved.

Thor the mighty god of thunder was travelling through the snowstorm in pursuit of his enemies, the Frost Giants. He heard the human voices calling from the forest.

a) He took pity on the two men and frightened off the wolves with his magical hammer. He demanded a beautiful carving as payment.

b) The Frost Giants killed the wolves and were about to attack the young man and his loyal slave. Thor strapped on the magical belt which doubled his strength and fought off the giants.

Thor then made a path to lead the astonished pair back to the village.

Stage Six

Say how the story ends.

a) The young man produced a fantastic carving of Thor fighting the Frost Giants. People came from miles around to see it because they believed that it had magical powers.

b) The young man carved the story of Thor's adventures in runes. The stone was so large that it could not be moved. Only he and the slave knew of its magical powers.

As a reward for his bravery, the slave was given his freedom.

HOW SHALL I END THE STORY?

Historical story
Vocabulary bank 2

apprentice	frozen	skis
assistance	furs	slave
		slavery
battle	howling	sledge
blizzard		snow drift
brave, bravery	learning	snow shoes
	longhouse	snowstorm
carver	loyal	stone
carvings		strength
chieftain	magic hammer	
craft		task
craftsman	Odin, most important	test
	Viking god	Thor, god of thunder,
defeat	owe	had red hair and a
		beard
famous	pillars	
forest		victorious
foster family	repay	
freedom, freed	reward	wilderness
Frost Giants, enemies	runes	wolves
of the gods	rune-master	

My own words

Wrong Place, Right Time

Chris heard the end-of-break bell ring clearly but booted the soccer ball regardless. It was a lousy kick and the ball veered wildly off to the side and smashed through the boiler-shed window. He looked around in horror but no one else seemed to have noticed; the other children were already lined up patiently waiting to return to class. He wanted to get his ball back; it was brand new and there was no way that he was going to leave it in that grubby old shed. He grabbed his protesting friend George and roughly pulled him behind the wall.

'The shed's out of bounds!' gasped George. 'We'll get into heaps of trouble if the caretaker sees us. Plus we're late for class.'

'I don't care! I want my ball back. You keep watch and warn me if anyone is coming,' hissed Chris.

The shed was bolted but not locked. Chris doggedly dragged back the squeaky catch and heaved on the old warped door. George watched him disappear suddenly into the gloom and decided to follow him.

Inside there were sacks full of coal and dust floated hazily in the air. As his eyes became accustomed to the dark, George could see Chris carefully kicking aside shards of glass, gingerly retrieving his soccer ball.

'Drat! I've cut myself on some glass,' said Chris, sucking noisily at the wound on his palm. 'Why do little cuts always bleed so much?'

'Shh! Did you hear that?' whispered George.

Chris nodded. There was a faint cry coming from the back of the shed. Lessons forgotten, both boys peered cautiously over the musty old sacks. A mother cat lay on her side, protecting three scrawny kittens. She was so skinny that the boys could see her ribs and she just stared at them with dull eyes, not even bothering to move. The kittens were obviously very weak too and lay without making any noise.

'Poor thing,'said Chris. 'I guess she was shut in by accident. She must be absolutely starving.'

'What shall we do?' asked George. 'She doesn't look strong enough for us to move her.'

'First we have to get her some food and water. If she is OK then she will look after her kittens herself. Then we need to…OH BOTHER! Someone is calling us. We have to go back to class. We can pull the door to and duck around quickly to the boys' toilets. You can say that you were helping me to clean up this cut on my hand! Come on!'

Their teacher was not very impressed with their excuse and wanted to know why they were both covered in black dust. The two boys hardly noticed what was said because they were too busy thinking about the hungry cat and her kittens. When the lunch bell rang Chris surreptitiously joined the line for school dinners.

'What are you doing? You have sandwiches!' exclaimed George.

'Oh, they always have a couple of spare meals, so nobody will notice,' explained Chris. 'Plus it's fish and chips today so the cat should be really happy! I'll pay for it tomorrow out of my pocket money. You just go and get a bowl of water and meet me round by the shed. Make sure that no one sees you or we'll be in even more of a fix!'

Ten minutes later, both boys were crouched down behind the sacks watching the cat. She had lapped up most of the water and was now ravenously devouring the fish. She started to nuzzle her kittens but they were hardly responding.

'What should we do next?' asked George.

'YOU CAN JOLLY WELL COME OUT OF MY SHED!' shouted the irate caretaker who was scowling at them from the doorway. 'YOU KNOW THIS AREA IS OUT OF BOUNDS FOR PUPILS. YOU ARE GOING STRAIGHT TO THE HEADTEACHER.'

'But…there's this cat and…'

'NO EXCUSES!'

The boys had no option but to leave the cat and her kittens and follow the fuming caretaker.

The headteacher listened carefully to the caretaker and then asked the boys for their explanation. When at last they fell silent, the headteacher said, 'My, my, you have been busy!' So, let me review the situation…'

The boys glanced nervously at each other. They were so concerned about their new feline friend that they were not really worried about themselves.

'On the one hand we have a broken window; going into an out-of-bounds area – twice; skiving off lessons and taking a school dinner that you did not order. On the other we have a cat and a litter of kittens that would probably have died if you had not found them!'

The headteacher looked at the boys. 'I am puzzled why you did not just inform a teacher and save yourselves all this mess?'

'It is all my fault really,' said Chris, haltingly. 'I broke the window and made George get involved in the first place. Then we were just too busy thinking about the cat!'

'Well, you both need to apologise to the caretaker for going into his shed. You also need to write me three paragraphs about why it is wrong to go into an out-of-bounds area. Then you have to sort out how you are going to pay for the fish and chips and the broken window! I will explain to your class teacher what has been going on.'

'What about the cat and the kittens?' queried George anxiously.

'I think that you ought to contact the RSPCA and see if they can look after them until they are healthy again. What do you think should happen to them after that?' asked the headteacher.

'The cat doesn't have a collar so… maybe if no one claims her… we could have her as the school pet?' suggested Chris hopefully.

'That's a lovely idea but I'm afraid that it's just not feasible,' said the headteacher. 'We are not allowed to have school pets."

'Well, maybe we could advertise them in the school newsletter so they go to good homes!' piped up George.

'That sounds like a better option,' smiled the headteacher. 'Perhaps there is hope for the two of you yet!'

'Cool!' said the boys, grinning at each other in relief.

'Umm... Could we go back to the shed to see if the kittens are OK?'

Understanding the grammar and punctuation

Adverbs

Adverbs explain things for us.

How (in what way)
ravenously, hopefully, patiently

When (at what time)
first, next, tomorrow

Where (in which place)
there, behind, here

How often things happen
sometimes, hardly, never

Adverbs and suffixes

A lot of adverbs end with the suffix 'ly'.

carefully

quickly

hardly

noisily

But not all of them!

fast

high

Paragraphs

A paragraph is a group of sentences about one idea.

You begin a new paragraph to introduce a new idea, a different place, time or character and the next event in the story.

You begin a new paragraph every time a new character speaks.

'The shed's out of bounds!' gasped George.

'I don't care! I want my ball back. You keep watch and warn me if anyone is coming,' hissed Chris.

Adverbs

Read these sentences. Underline the verbs and circle the adverbs.

1. The ball veered wildly off to the side.

2. George appeared suddenly.

3. The teacher listened carefully to the answer.

4. The class was waiting patiently in a line.

Add the suffix 'ly' to these adjectives to form adverbs.

clear _____   sweet _____

cautious _____   heavy _____

bad _____   nervous _____

loud _____   harsh _____

Write four sentences of your own using adverbs.

1. _____

2. _____

3. _____

4. _____

Choose an adverb from the ones below to complete each of these sentences.

increasingly   suddenly   immediately   quickly

1. He ran _____ to catch the cat.

2. _____, I saw the angry figure in the door.

3. He was _____ worried about the missing child.

4. She knew _____ what was wrong.

Paragraphs

Reorder these sentences so that they become the opening paragraph of a school adventure story.

The pottery for the art exhibition somersaulted through the air in slow motion and smashed sickeningly into the floor.

The pounding footsteps behind her were gaining and the bullies' taunts rang in her ears.

The headteacher glared at her in fury.

In the split second that she threw a frightened glance over her shoulder, she collided with someone emerging from a classroom.

The frantic girl ran as fast as she could along the deserted corridor.

_____

_____

_____

_____

_____

_____

_____

_____

_____

_____

Read the phrases below. They are all examples of paragraph connectives used to show the passing of time. Choose a book and make a list of any other time connectives you can find. Write them here.

All of a sudden...   *The next moment...*   *A few hours later...*   *Soon after that...*

Helpful hints for writing a school adventure story

✦ Your adventure is set in a school, so make sure that you include a few details about the school to make it seem real. However, do not include too much detail or it will spoil your fast moving plot!

✦ Make your characters ordinary people. This helps to create a contrast between the ordinary people and the unusual things that happen to them in the story.

✦ Use exclamation marks and capital letters to make certain parts of the story stand out and to make events seem exciting.

✦ Remember to use paragraphs. Begin new paragraphs with adverbs of time to add to the sense of a fast moving plot; for example:

tomorrow, sometimes, firstly, finally

✦ Dialogue can give the reader insight into the the situation and the character's emotions. This saves you writing long descriptions!

✦ Show how the characters are changed by their adventure. Maybe they make new friends; maybe they stop being nasty to someone; maybe they learn a new skill.

✦ Include an emergency or an evil villain in your story. Chases and daring rescues build up the tension in the story.

✦ Leave the reader in suspense with a series of cliffhangers and twisted plots.

✦ At the end of the story the main characters should triumph over the difficulty they faced. There should be a happy ending.

School adventure story
Scaffold 1

You are going to write a school adventure story.
To help plan your story, use the framework below.
Choose one option from each stage.

Stage One

Choose the characters for your story.

a) Two school friends.

b) A brother and sister.

Stage Two

Start your story with a good beginning.

A freak gust of wind, a loud whooshing sound and the new stunt kite spiralled out of control and crashed into the top of the tallest tree.

a) The children were horrified. They were not allowed to climb the trees at school.

b) The children were horrified. The stunt kite belonged to their teacher and they would be in big trouble if they lost or damaged it.

Stage Three

Set the scene for the story.

The children were competing in the school kite flying competition the following day. They had to get the stunt kite down from the tree.

a) One of the children was a really good gymnast. He/she decided to climb up quickly and retrieve the kite, while the other kept guard. They hoped that the teachers wouldn't see them.

b) Both children were scared of heights, so they drew sticks to see who would have to climb up and fetch the kite.

Stage Four

Give the characters a problem.

The climber got entangled in the kite line and couldn't get down. The tree was very spindly at the top and it looked as if the branches would give way at any moment. The climber couldn't hold on for much longer.

a) The headteacher caught sight of them and came running out to see what was happening.

b) The child on the ground realised that he/she had to raise the alarm.

Stage Five

Say how the problem is solved.

The tree was unable to support the weight of anyone else and the school ladder was too short to reach that high. The whole school came out to watch what was going on.

a) The fire engine was called out to rescue the stranded climber. It arrived with sirens blaring.

b) All the fire trucks were busy with a fire, so a rescue helicopter was called to winch the climber to safety.

Stage Six

Say how the story ends.

The children had a lot of explaining to do. Luckily the kite was undamaged and they were still allowed to take part in the stunt kite competition.

a) They won first prize and ended up with their photographs in the local newspaper twice in one week.

b) The school started to take the children for lessons on the rock-climbing wall at the local leisure centre. They wanted to make sure that they learned how to climb safely.

School adventure story
Vocabulary bank 1

acrobat
aerobatics display
audience

branch, bough
bravery

cheered, applauded
climbed
competition

determined
dramatic
drew lots
dropped like a stone

effort
emergency
exhaustion

fluttered
flying
frightened

glanced
great height

headteacher
heaved
helicopter
hero, heroine

newspaper
nylon line

reporter
rescue services
rope ladder

scaled
scared
screamed
silence, mute
slipped
spindly
stunt kite

tail
tangled, entangle

waited breathlessly
watched in horror
weak at the knees
winch
witness

My own words

School adventure story
Scaffold 2

You are going to write a school adventure story.
To help plan your story, use the framework below.
Choose one option from each stage, or two if the stage is in sections.

Stage One

Choose the characters for your story.

a) Two boys.

b) A girl and her best friend.

They were going on a school trip to a dinosaur museum.

Stage Two

Start your story with a good beginning.

They were holding real dinosaur bones! This was the best school museum trip ever! It was very crowded though, so they had to keep an eye on their group.

a) Some of the dinosaur models looked real because they moved and made sounds.

b) The T-Rex model looked as though it was running after you because you could feel the ground shaking.

Stage Three

Set the scene for the story.

The other school groups had moved on but the two friends were so engrossed with the dinosaurs that they did not notice.

a) All at once they looked up and realised that they were surrounded by strangers.

b) An unruly bunch of children from another school surged past and the two characters were squashed up against a dinosaur display.

Stage Four

Give the characters a problem.

The friends realised that they were lost. They were worried that no one would notice and the bus would leave without them.

a) One child panicked and accidentally knocked over an enormous dinosaur skeleton. Bones flew everywhere.

b) They darted through the nearest door and found themselves in the gruesome specimen room where all sorts of creatures were preserved.

Stage Five

Say how the problem is solved.

The children had no idea what to do. Luckily…

a) a kindly security guard took them to where all the close circuit television screens were monitored. They spotted their school group on one of the screens and made an announcement over the intercom.

b) the museum dinosaur specialist came to their rescue. They were taken to the Lost Property desk, getting a special museum tour on the way.

Stage Six

Say how the story ends.

Their teacher had just done a head count for the sixth time and was very worried because there were two pupils missing. Just as the alarm is about to be sounded … the children turn up.

a) The museum gave them free tickets so they could come back and finish their visit properly.

b) The teacher was very relieved to see them and spent the whole journey back to school checking the number of pupils on the bus.

School adventure story
Vocabulary bank 2

adventure
alarm
announcement
anxious, fearful

boisterous
bones, fossils, relics

close-circuit television
coach, minibus
cold sweat
crowd, mass

dinosaur
disorientated
displays, stands
distracted
dread

exhibition
exhilarating

expert, specialist

friends, companion

initiative
intercom

location, place
lost property

missing, lose, mislaid
memento, memory
model
monitored, watched
museum

officer

panic

relieved, reassured
rescue
reunited

screens
shake
security
sigh of relief
strangers

tearful
trembling
trip, outing, excursion

unknown, unfamiliar
unruly

wandered
weeping, sobbing
worried, worrying

My own words

Hansel and Gretel

Cast of characters
Stepmother Ghost (SMG)
Hansel
Gretel
Witch

Act 1 – Scene 1

(*There is a clearing in the middle of a forest. A cottage made out of sweets and cakes stands stage right. There is the sound of hungry wolves howling in the distance. From behind a tree steps **Stepmother Ghost**. She steps slowly forward looking about her. She sees the cottage and laughs horribly. **Stepmother Ghost** comes to the front of stage left and addresses the audience.*)

SMG: Yes, I am dead. Look at my bones – dead from starvation. Oh, I got rid of my stepchildren Hansel and Gretel, but it was too late. If only I had done it earlier, there would have been enough food for me. Their father still lives, but his time is short. The fool! I said to him 'You are being very stupid. Take the children into the forest and leave them.' 'How can I do that to my children?' he whimpered. 'Perhaps someone will rescue them,' I told him. As if I cared! He is too soft.

(*Stepmother Ghost* moves to stage centre.)

Oh I know how they got back the first time. Hansel dropped white stones all the way into the forest and they just followed them back. The second time he used breadcrumbs. Breadcrumbs! Of course they have been eaten by the birds. The children have been wandering around this forest for days, eating berries and nuts. In the meantime, I writhe at home in hunger and die, doomed to wander as a ghost.

(*She bends forward and speaks in a stage whisper, pointing to the cottage.*)

My revenge is there. They are coming. I shall watch with glee.

(*She puts her fingers to her lips and creeps back behind the tree.*)

Scene 2

(*Hansel* and *Gretel* enter.)

Gretel: I am so tired, Hansel.

Hansel: This is a good place to stop. You look so sad. Don't worry about father. Somehow, things will be all right.

Gretel: Look, Hansel. Look, a cottage!

Hansel: Gretel – it is made out of sweets and cakes. The stones of the walls are buns. Oh, I am so hungry. Shall I take just one little one?

Gretel: Of course. I shall take one too.

(*The children* *take a bun off the wall of the cottage. While they are eating them, an old lady, who is really a* *witch, comes out of the door.*)

Witch: Hello, dear children. What are you doing?

Gretel: Oh, I am so sorry. My brother and I are lost and we haven't had anything to eat for days. We saw your buns…

Hansel: It wasn't my sister's fault. Please forgive us for taking these buns off your lovely house and eating them. We haven't done any damage.

Witch: Ssh, Ssh, little dears. I'm not angry. You poor sweet things. Come inside and I will look after you. Come along, my pretty pets, come in, come in.

(*As if in a daze,* **Hansel** *and* **Gretel** *follow the* **Witch** *into the cottage.* **Stepmother Ghost** *steps out from behind the tree, points to the cottage, licks her lips, rubs her tummy and cackles with glee.*)

Act 2 Scene 1

(*It is inside the* **Witch's** *cottage. There is a large oven stage left and a cage stage right. The* **Witch** *is stirring something on the oven.* **Stepmother Ghost** *is standing watching. No one can see her.* **Hansel** *and* **Gretel** *enter.*)

Witch: Ah, there you are, my pretties. Did you sleep well?

Hansel: Oh yes, thank you.

Gretel: You are so kind. Is there anything we can do for you?

Witch: I am cooking you a big, BIG breakfast. Lay the table, little Gretel. Hansel, come closer to me please, so that I can see you.

(**Hansel** *moves closer to the* **Witch**. *She grabs him and drags him to the cage and locks him in.* **Gretel** *stares at her.*)

Gretel: What are you doing?

Hansel: Why have you locked me in this cage?

Witch: You are silly children. Did you think I was going to give you all my food for nothing? I am going to keep you here my dears until Hansel is fat enough to make into a tasty stew. You won't run away Gretel, because you will want to stay with your brother. Now do as I say and it will all be over much quicker. Gretel, you will help me because I can't see very well. Give your brother this food.

(*The* **Witch** *piles up a plate of food.* **Gretel** *who is in great distress, puts the food near the cage so that* **Hansel** *can eat it.*)

                  Hansel, everyday you will poke your finger through the bars of the cage so that I can feel how fat you are getting. Gretel, go and fetch some water.

Hansel: Do as she says Gretel. She must really be a witch and I don't know what she can do. Don't worry, we'll think of something.

Witch: Think away, stupid boy. Eat now, eat up and get good and juicy.

(The **Witch** crows with laughter. **Gretel** picks up a bucket and, crying, exits. The **Witch** feels her way to a chair and sits, rocking and licking her lips. **Hansel** curls up on the floor of the cage and puts his arms over his head.)

SMG: Suffer you greedy children. Suffer and die like me.

(There is a roll of thunder and the stage darkens.)

Scene 2

(The **Witch's** kitchen. **Gretel** is kneeling by the cage. **Stepmother Ghost** watches.)

Hansel: Where is she, Gretel?

Gretel: Creeping around outside. Now Hansel, only eat enough to keep yourself alive. I have stolen this chicken bone. When she wants to feel your finger, poke the bone through the bars of the cage and she'll think you're not fat enough to eat yet. This will give us time to plan our escape.

(The **Witch** enters.)

Witch: Hoi there my girl. What are you doing?

Gretel: Giving my brother some food to fatten him up.

Witch: Good girl, good girl. Let me feel how fat he is now.

(**Hansel** pokes the chicken bone through the bars of the cage. The **Witch** feels the bone.)

Witch: You still seem so thin. It is going to take longer than I thought. Gretel, you and I shall make some bread to mop up his juices when he's ready. I put the oven on this morning.

(The **Witch** hobbles to the oven.)

SMG: You foolish old woman. They are tricking you.

(**Stepmother Ghost** tries everything to gain the **Witch's** attention, without success.)

Witch: Gretel, come here.

(**Gretel** goes over to her and the **Witch** opens the door of the oven.)

Crawl in there and see if it is hot enough.

Gretel: I don't want to. You might cook me and eat me.

Witch: Don't be silly girl. Look, let me go in and show you how easy it is to get in and out.

(The **Witch** crawls into the oven. **Stepmother Ghost** screams 'No!' **Gretel** slams the door of the oven shut.)

Witch: Let me out! Let me out!

Gretel: I'll never let you out, you are a wicked old witch.

Hansel: Unlock the cage Gretel.

(*Gretel unlocks the cage.*)

Witch: I'll tell you where my treasure is if you let me out. My treasure has always remained a secret. I won't eat you.

Hansel: We don't believe you've got any treasure.

Witch: Go and look under my bed if you don't believe me.

(*Hansel and Gretel look at each other and rush off. There is a moment's pause. Then cries of joy are heard off stage.*)

Witch: Help! I'm cooking! Help!

SMG: (*running forward to audience*) Save her. Don't let those stupid children escape with her treasure. Did I die in vain?

(*She goes into the audience, while the Witch is screaming in the oven, she goes up to members of the audience shouting at them to save the witch. As Stepmother Ghost reaches the back of the auditorium, there is a final screech from the Witch.*)

SMG : She's dead! Oh no! Here comes her ghost!

(*The ghost of the Witch comes out from the oven and sees the Stepmother Ghost*)

Witch: It is all your fault. You should have killed them properly when you had the chance. Now they have my treasure and I am dead! I shall haunt you for eternity for causing all this trouble.

SMG : Don't… don't come near me!

(*The Witch leaps from the stage and, shrieking, chases Stepmother Ghost out of the auditorium. There is a short silence. Hansel and Gretel creep onto the stage carrying a treasure chest. They put it down stage centre and look around them. They realise the Witch is dead. They hug each other. They open the treasure chest and light from the treasure reflects in their faces.*)

Hansel: Gretel, we are rich beyond our imaginations.

Gretel: How will we take it back to father, Hansel? We must rescue him.

Hansel: Now we are rich, we can pay someone to take us home. Oh Gretel, our troubles are over.

Gretel: What about our Stepmother?

Hansel: We will forgive her, Gretel.

(*There is the sound of a faint 'No – oh no' backstage from Stepmother Ghost and we hear the Witch yelling 'Here I come' and Stepmother Ghost crying 'Leave me alo-o-o-one'*).

We shall live happily ever after.

(*The light on stage fades, leaving a spotlight on Hansel and Gretel. The curtains close*).

Understanding the grammar and punctuation

Sentences

A simple sentence can have any number of words, but every sentence must have three things:

1. A subject.

2. A verb or verb phrase (a phrase is a few words that does the same job in the sentence as one word).

3. An object or a complement.

'I am cooking you a big, BIG breakfast.'

I is the subject because the sentence is about what *I* does.

am cooking is the verb, because it is what *I* did.

breakfast is the object.

...

'You are a wicked old witch.'

You is the subject of the sentence.

are is the verb of the sentence.

a wicked old witch is the complement of the sentence.

A complement of a sentence is used when you want to say how the subject is feeling or say more about the subject. For example:

The witch was old and ugly.

old and ugly say something more about the witch, so it is a complement.

Punctuation

There are many types of sentences. All sentences begin with a capital letter.

Most sentences end with a full stop.

If the sentence asks a question, it ends with a question mark (?). For example:

'What about our Stepmother?'

If the sentence gives an order that almost seems to be shouted, it ends with an exclamation mark (!) For example:

Let me out!

If the sentence is an exclamation, that is, it seems to be a surprise or a shock, it ends with an exclamation mark (!) For example:

I'm cooking!

Name

Sentences

Look at this list of words. Circle the **verbs**.

just   know   do   we   eat   today   crusts   children   are
food   why   tell   stupid   want   slowly   die   starvation   food
be   shared   four   act   take   out   forest   leave   found

Look at these phrases. Circle the **verb phrases**.

going to die – in my pocket – will show – Father and Stepmother – go to sleep –
don't worry – a good place – cut down – our fires – be able to –
small pieces of wood – we'll go

A 'subject' is what a sentence is about. Underline the **subject** in these sentences.

1. Wolves will eat us.

2. I am so frightened.

3. The stones of the walls are buns.

An object is what the subject does something to. Underline the **object** in these sentences:

1. We can save our own lives.

2. I shall pick up lots of white stones.

3. I'll make a little fire.

Now write four sentences of your own. Circle the verbs and underline the subject in each one.

_____

_____

_____

_____

Capitals, fullstops, question and exclamation marks

The following text does not have any capital letters or full stops.
Try and read it to a partner!

now Hansel only eat enough to keep yourself alive I have stolen this chicken bone when she wants to feel your finger poke the bone through the bars of the cage and she'll think you're not fat enough to eat yet this will give us time to plan our escape

Now put in the capital letters and full stops. Read it again – does it make sense now?

The stepmother has written a letter to the father. Correct all the mistakes in it.

Do you want us all to die! Let them starve? Take them into the woods and leave them or I will scream? Why won't you do as I say! I have been a good wife to you haven't I? There is never enough food. Can't you see I am starving! I want food, I want food?

Decide whether the following need question marks (?) or exclamation marks (!).

You fool

How can stones show us the way home

*Get in the oven **now***

The crumbs have gone

What will you do

Be quiet

Where is she going

What shall we do

Write five sentences of your own. Make at least one end with a question mark and one with an exclamation mark.

_____

_____

_____

_____

Helpful hints for writing a playscript

✦ Don't have too many characters. List your characters at the top of the page; for example:

> Hansel
> Gretel
> Father
> Stepmother
> Witch

✦ Make your script simple. Divide your script into big parts called 'Acts'. Then divide the acts into smaller parts called 'Scenes'.

✦ Write the opening scene. Try to imagine what it would look like on a stage; for example:

Act Two. Scene One.

(It is inside the Witch's cottage. There is a large oven stage left and a cage stage right. The Witch is stirring something on the oven. Stepmother Ghost is standing watching. No one can see her. Hansel and Gretel enter.)

✦ Next, write the 'dialogue'. The dialogue is what the actors have to say. Write the name of the character who is going to speak on the left hand side of the page, leave a gap and then write what the character says. Keep what the character says in lines that start at the same place; for example:

Witch: *Ah, there you are my pretties. Did you sleep well?*

Hansel: *Oh yes, thank you.*

Gretel: *You are so kind. Is there anything we can do for you?*

✦ Remember to include 'stage directions'. These are instructions for the director of the play, the actor or the people who work backstage on lighting, costume and sound; for example:

(Hansel moves closer to the Witch.)

✦ Think of interesting things for your characters to do. What exciting things happen to them?

✦ Make each scene end in a way that will make the audience want to know what happens next.

✦ Make sure you have a good ending.

A playscript
Scaffold 1 – The Frog Prince

You are going to write a playscript.
To help plan your playscript, use the framework below.
Choose one option from each stage.

Stage One

Introduce the characters and set the scene. This will be your dialogue for Act 1, Scene 1.

Characters (list these at the top of your play): A princess, her father the king, a frog.

The princess was playing by herself with a ball near a:

a) pond;   b) lake;   c) well.

She was talking to herself as she played.

Stage Two

Give the characters a plan/a change/an adventure. This will be your dialogue for Act 1, Scene 2.

The ball fell into the pond/lake/well. The princess was very upset. A frog jumped out of the pond/lake/well. The princess told the frog that if he got the ball back for her, she would give the frog:

a) a necklace;

b) a crown;

c) a bracelet.

Stage Three

Start the characters off on their adventure. This will be your dialogue for Act 1, Scene 3.

The frog said he didn't want a necklace/crown/bracelet. He wanted:

a) to eat from the princess's plate;

b) to sleep in the princess's bed;

c) to be the princess's friend and companion.

The princess agreed. The frog collected the ball for the princess.

Stage Four

Give the characters a problem. This will be your dialogue for Act 2, Scene 1.

The princess hated frogs. She thought they were ugly and slimy. The frog appeared in the palace so that the princess could keep her promise. The princess broke her promise. Her father, the king, was very cross with her and made her keep her promise. The princess:

a) was so unkind to the frog that she made him cry;

b) threw the frog against a wall and hurt him;

c) was very upset, but the frog was kind to her.

Stage Five

The problem is solved. This will be your dialogue for Act 3, Scene 1.

The princess felt so sorry for the frog that she:

a) kissed him;

b) stroked him;

c) told him she loved him.

Stage Six

Conclude the playscript. This will be your dialogue for Act 3, Scene 2.

The frog:

a) turned into a handsome prince, married the princess and they lived happily ever after;

b) turned into a handsome prince and rode off looking for a nicer princess;

c) turned into a handsome prince with magic powers. He turned the princess into a frog.

A playscript
Vocabulary bank 1

apologise

glittering

noble

beastly

gobble

playmates

beautiful

golden ball

refuse

charms

jewels

revenge

constant companion

croak

keep your word

snore

knobbly

spoilt

deep

diamonds

leaped

temper tantrum

dribble

lonely

favourite

magnificent

forgive

My own words

A playscript
Scaffold 2 – Jack and the beanstalk

You are going to write a playscript.
To help plan your playscript, use the framework below.
Choose one option from each stage.

Stage One

Introduce the characters and set the scene. This will be your dialogue for Act 1, Scene 1.

Characters: Jack, Jack's mother, a man, a giant. (Write these at the top of your playscript.)

Jack lived with his mother. They were so poor they had nothing to eat. Jack's mother told Jack to take their beloved cow to the market and:

a) sell it for money;

b) sell it for food;

c) sell it for a bag of grain.

Stage Two

Give the characters a plan/a change/an adventure. This will be your dialogue for Act 1, Scene 2.

On the way to market, Jack met a man who offered to buy the cow for magic beans. Jack sold him the cow and went home to his mother who:

a) threw the beans out of the window;

b) was so angry with Jack that she refused to talk to him. Jack planted the beans in the garden.

c) was so angry with Jack that she threw him out of the house. Jack planted the beans in the woods near his house.

Stage Three

Start the characters off on their adventure. This will be your dialogue for Act 1, Scene 1.

The next morning the beans had grown into a giant beanstalk. Jack climbed up the beanstalk and found a giant's house. Jack hid in a cupboard. The giant came in and:

a) began to count gold coins into giant bags of money;

b) listened to a golden harp making beautiful music;

c) played with a hen who could lay golden eggs.

Stage Four

Give the characters a problem. This will be your dialogue for Act 2, Scene 1.

The giant fell asleep. Jack stole the bags of money/golden harp/hen. As he ran away, the money/golden harp/hen called out to the giant and woke him up.

a) Jack climbed down the beanstalk with the giant climbing down after him.

b) Jack climbed down the beanstalk with the giant climbing down after him, but the giant's weight was bending the beanstalk.

c) Jack climbed down the beanstalk with the giant climbing down after him shouting 'FEE, FIE, FOE, FUM, I SMELL THE BLOOD OF AN ENGLISHMAN.'

Stage Five

The problem is solved. This will be your dialogue for Act 3, Scene 1.

a) Jack got to the bottom of the beanstalk, yelled to his mother to get an axe. Jack cut the beanstalk down. The giant fell and was killed.

b) Jack got to the bottom of the beanstalk just as the beanstalk collapsed under the giant's weight. The giant was killed.

c) Jack got to the bottom of the beanstalk and set fire to the beanstalk. The giant was killed.

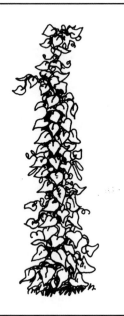

Stage Six

Conclude the playscript. This will be your dialogue for Act 3, Scene 2.

Jack and his mother now had the bags of money/the golden harp/the hen who laid golden eggs. They were rich.

a) Jack went to market and bought back his beloved cow.

b) Jack found another magic bean and decided to plant it.

c) Jack and his mother decided to farm properly. They went to market, bought clothes, food, animals – and lots of beans to grow.

A playscript
Vocabulary bank 2

ancient	hack	rhapsody
awake	heavy	
	high as the sky	screamed
bough	humble	send to Coventry
		smashed
emaciated	ignoramus	starvation
enchanted		strange
enormous	leaping flames	
		thundering
furious	million	ton
		trunk
galore	never ending	tumble
gargantuan		tumbledown
	poverty	

My own words

A holiday with my family

CHAPTER ONE

My family is very normal really. We live in a normal house in a normal road. My dad has a normal job as a builder. My mum works in our normal school as a classroom assistant. My little sister, Annie, is the normal pain in the neck. I am the most normal nine-year-old boy I have ever met and my gran, who lives with us, looks like a normal, sweet, grey-haired old lady. She does smoke and drinks loads of beer, but as she says, it's normal for old people to have a few habits for young people to disapprove of. It was quite normal for all of us to be sitting round the kitchen table looking miserable, too.

'We're not moving from this table until we've decided where we're going for our holidays and that's that!' my dad, Jim, said, glaring at us. He's a big bloke, my dad. He's over six feet tall with massive arms covered in tattoos he got when he was in the navy. Gran lit another fag.

'The trouble is,' she sighed, 'that we can't think of a holiday that would suit all of us.' She brushed some ash off her blue cardigan.

'I'd like to do something different this year anyway,' said Mum, who was as little as Dad was big. We sat in silence, staring at the remains of breakfast on the table. I was thinking that what I'd really like to do was to learn how to brew beer for Gran. She and I were good mates and my parents were always moaning about the money she spent on beer. If I could learn how to brew it at home, I could stop at least some of the many arguments my parents told me were quite normal in families.

Then, out of the blue, the idea was in my head! I couldn't believe how good it was, so I took a good long look at it. My face must have reflected some of its brilliance because my sister whined.

'Mum, Sam's pulling stupid faces at me.'

'Oh stop it, Sam,' Mum said, without bothering to find out what was really going on, which was quite normal.

'No, look everyone. I've got it, I've got it!' I jumped out of my chair and began pacing around the table. 'Why don't we all think of what we would really – and I mean really – want to do. There are holiday places you can go to where you can try

out new things – they have activities and lessons and things. I've seen them on those holiday programmes on telly. It might be something you've always wanted to try, Mum, or something you would like to learn, Dad. Even Annie might find something to stop her whingeing.'

'SAM!' Mum and Dad said together, warning me off my attack on Annie.

'You know, Sam,' Gran said, 'I think you have found the solution. That's brilliant!' She lifted her tea cup and toasted me. 'I've always wanted to learn football skills. You run rings round me when we play. I'd like to learn how to give you a bit of a challenge.'

'Don't be ridiculous,' Mum said. 'A woman of your age doing football skills!'

'Why not?' Dad cried, 'It might surprise you to know, Carol' (that's my mum's name) 'that I have always wanted to learn how to do flower arranging'. We stared at him in amazement. He was going very red. 'Just because Gran is a bit older than us and just because I'm a bloke, doesn't mean that we always have to do what is expected of us. I like Sam's idea.'

'Well, Jim,' said Mum, 'in that case I might have a surprise for you lot too. I've always wanted to learn how to ride a motorbike.' We all cheered and Dad gave Mum a hug.

'That's my girl,' he cried. 'I can just see you roaring down the road on a huge motorbike, dressed in leathers.' Mum went pink and gave him a push.

'What do you two want to do?' asked Gran, looking at Annie and me. I told them about wanting to brew beer for Gran, which didn't seem to make anyone happy except Gran. Annie, typically, had the most boring idea in the family. She wanted to learn how to do first aid.

CHAPTER TWO

That is how, a few months later, we were starting our first day at The Wonder Wood Activity Centre. The centre looked great. Everyone stayed in wooden chalets scattered around an enormous wood. There was an indoor area where you could buy things, eat at different sorts of restaurants and cafes and play lots of sports. It also offered courses in all the things we had chosen. That morning, we were all excited as we agreed where to meet for lunch, said goodbye to each other and set off for our first lessons.

To be honest, I wasn't feeling very hungry a few hours later as the waitress put my favourite pizza down in front of me. My family didn't seem quite normal either. They all said that they had had a great time and the course was just what they wanted, but Mum, Dad, Gran and Annie were, well, a bit too happy. It was almost as if they were putting it on a bit. I certainly wasn't going to tell them about my morning. The holiday had been my idea so I wasn't going to spoil it. The trouble was, I was the only child on the beer making course, everyone else was a grown-up. There had also been a bit of bother about someone my age making beer until I pointed out to them that I wouldn't be drinking it. What was worse, though, was that all the others on the course knew a lot about beer making already and I hadn't got a clue. I couldn't see any real harm in sneaking out a load of equipment and ingredients to practise with in my room back at the chalet. No one would ever know. Still, the thought put me off my pizza somehow.

That night, when everyone had gone to bed, I read through the instructions given to me in the lesson that morning. I set up the glass jars and tubes I had borrowed. I carefully poured in some powder, called hops, added some sugar and water and sat down to watch what would happen. After an hour, nothing had changed, so I went to sleep, happily thinking of how impressed the other members on my course were going to be with my knowledge about beer making.

The next morning was bright and sunny and I leaped out of bed early so that no one would come in to wake me up and find my beer experiment laid out in my room. At half past nine, I took a cup of tea in to Gran. She was sitting up in bed wearing my Arsenal tee shirt and taking out her curlers.

'How's the footie going, Gran?' I beamed. She glared back.

'It's got some stupid rules, hasn't it?' she said.

'Like what?' I asked.

'Oh, like silly cards being waved at you just because you gently push some little squirt over.' She sipped her tea.

'Gran, that's a foul. You're not supposed to be rough you know,' I frowned.

'Don't worry, Sam. I'll behave myself today,' she grinned. As I left her room I thought I heard her add, 'So long as the knee biters don't get in my way.' I decided to ignore her comment as there was the roar of an engine outside our chalet. I raced to the front door and flung it open. A pile of mud flew through the air and smacked me in the face. Wiping my eyes, I saw Mum, in jogging pants, a pink tee shirt and a large black helmet, skidding through the trees on a massive motor bike, churning up

mud and leaves, before sliding round a corner. Another holiday maker shouted something very rude at my Mum, then the sound of the engine disappeared into the distance. I had a moment's feeling of panic until I remembered Dad's flower arranging and my sister's first aid. They were peaceful pastimes, nothing could go wrong there. So with an easy heart, I cleaned myself up and went off for my next lesson.

CHAPTER THREE

That night there was trouble brewing as well as my beer. My room smelled disgusting and foam had built up in one of the jars, but it was my family who were really bubbling. Gran, apparently, had locked herself in her room. We could hear a football being kicked furiously against a wall. Mum's head was wrapped in a tangle of bandages and her arms were strapped to her sides with more bandages. She was shouting at Dad and Annie, but she looked so funny they were both trying really hard not to laugh at her.

'You will take these bandages off me this minute,' Mum yelled at my sister.

'But Mum, you fell off your motorbike, you were injured. I am only trying to help,' Annie said.

'I only got a few bruises. How dare you wrap me up like this and then refuse to take them off? Jim, take these bandages off me now!' Dad straightened his face and said, 'Not until you say I can keep my flower arrangement in our room.'

'Flower arrangement! Flower arrangement!' Mum was beside herself with rage now. 'How can a tree trunk, dustbins and a pile of bricks be a flower arrangement?' she screamed.

Dad leaned back in his chair. 'I've decided to do a large scale arrangement, Carol. You just don't understand my artistic abilities.'

I think Mum would have thrown herself at him as a bandaged missile if I hadn't stepped in. I unwrapped the bandages from Mum and threw them at Annie. Mum stormed into my parents' bedroom and, judging from the swear words that were not normal for her, fell over Dad's flower arrangement. Dad calmly picked up a chainsaw he had obviously brought from home without us noticing and walked out of the chalet. I turned to Annie but I made a BIG mistake. I told her to find someone else to practise her first aid on. Stupidly, I took no notice of the big smile spreading across her face.

CHAPTER FOUR

I was feeling pleased with myself as I made my way back to our chalet the following afternoon. I had been able to join in with the discussions on temperatures, fermenting and bottling with the grown-ups on the beer making course. My family had decided to get together that night to make peace over a family meal. It looked like the holiday was going to be a big success and it was all down to me.

Lovely smells of a roast dinner greeted me as I entered the chalet. Mum was looking happy and pretty, apart from the odd cuts and bruises. Gran seemed positively glowing in my Arsenal shirt and her football boots as she downed her pint of beer. Dad had moved his flower arrangement outside the chalet. He was happily walking round it, looking up at the branches and adjusting the bricks and dustbins artistically arranged amongst them. Even Annie seemed like a nice, normal person as she neatly wound up rolls of bandages. As the twilight settled, my family sat down to eat together. The only thing that wasn't quite normal for us was that we were all being polite to each other and we were all happy at the same time.

Just as we finished pudding, there was a knock on the chalet door. It was one of the Wonder Wood Activity Centre's organisers. He seemed a bit nervous, so Dad got him a chair, Mum

poured him a cup of coffee and Gran offered him a cigarette. We were all talking at once, saying how much we were enjoying the holiday, when he held up one hand for silence and tugged at his tie with the other.

'I'm afraid there have been some complaints,' he stuttered.

'Complaints?' queried Mum. 'What do you mean?'

'Well,' said the organiser, pointing at Gran. 'For example, I'm sorry to say that the football coach won't have you anymore. The parents of the boys say that if you continue they will take their boys off the course.'

Mum turned to Gran. 'What on earth have you been up to?' she asked.

I hid my face in my hands.

'Lot of sissies. Is it my fault they make such a fuss every time they fall over?' Gran muttered.

'Well, apparently, they are falling over because you have been pushing, kicking and punching them,' said the organiser.

'How could you?' gasped Mum, staring at Gran.

'That's not all though,' the organiser turned to Mum. 'The motorcyclists won't have you on their course either. They say you're a danger to everyone in the entire centre.'
'What a cheek!' Mum replied. 'I may have made a few people jump out of the way, but they should look where they are going.'

'Really, Carol. I'm ashamed of you,' said Dad.

'You, Jim, will have to leave the Centre tomorrow,' said the organiser. ' You've been cutting down trees and that is strictly against the rules.'

'Dad!' Annie wailed, 'You've spoiled our holiday.'

'And as for you,' the organiser now turned his gaze to my sister. 'You are lucky that old Mrs Turner hasn't called in the police to arrest you for tripping her over and then bandaging her up so that she couldn't move for two hours.'

'Annie!' We all shouted.

'It seems', I said, looking round furiously at my family, 'that all of you have behaved disgracefully. You have ruined my idea of a perfect holiday for us all. None of you, none of you, are at all normal. It is lucky for you that I am normal and that there is at least one person in this family that has not done anything wrong.'

It was simply bad timing that my beer experiment exploded at that precise moment. We had to pay for the broken windows and for redecorating the room of course. It is six months since we came home from our holiday and I haven't had any pocket money yet. No one will listen to any of my many, brilliant ideas either. Still, it is quite normal for a genius to be ignored by his family.

Understanding the grammar and punctuation

Clauses

A clause is a group of words that has a subject and a verb in it. The clause tells us what happened to the subject.

Sentences are made up of clauses.

A simple sentence

A simple sentence has one clause in it.

My Gran smokes.

My Gran is the subject,

smokes is the verb.

A compound sentence

A compound sentence is made up of simple sentences joined together.

My Gran smokes and my Gran drinks.

My Gran smokes is a clause, but so is *My Gran drinks*. They both give important information. They are put in the same sentence by joining them with *and*.

A complex sentence

A complex sentence has a '**main clause**' (the part that gives us the most information and makes sense on its own) and a '**subordinate clause**'. The subordinate clause tells us less important information and does not make sense on its own.

My Gran smokes and drinks, but it's quite normal.

My Gran smokes and drinks is the main clause.
but it's quite normal is the subordinate clause.

Speech Punctuation

When anyone talks in a story, what they say is put inside speech marks.
For example:

'We're not moving from this table.'

Every time someone new speaks, they are given a new line on the page.

'Mum, Sam's pulling stupid faces at me.'

'Oh stop it, Sam,' Mum said.

Punctuation such as question marks and exclamation marks that belong to what the person said go inside the speech marks.

'Why not?' said Sam.

'SAM!' Mum and Dad said together.

Speech inside the speech marks begin with a capital letter unless a sentence has been interrupted.

'Oh stop it, Sam,' Mum said. 'You are making me cross.'

'Oh stop it Sam,' Mum said 'or I'll get cross.'

Types of sentences

A clause is a group of words that has a subject and a verb in it. Sentences are made up of clauses. A **simple sentence** has one clause. Underline the subject and circle the verb in each simple sentence below. One has been done for you.

1. <u>We</u> (drove) to London.
2. The boy carried the box to the shed.
3. We went to Spain on holiday.
4. Annie bandaged up her mother.
5. The plane trip took fifteen hours.

A **compound sentence** is made up of simple sentences joined by a conjunction. Underline the two clauses in each sentence below. Circle the conjunction. One has been done for you.

1. <u>I can play football</u> (and) <u>I can make paper aeroplanes</u>.
2. My mother can sing really well but my father can't sing at all!
3. The dog chased the cat and then he ran away.
4. I turned to Annie but I made a BIG mistake.
5. My sister is going to university because she wants to be a doctor.

A **complex sentence** has a main clause and a subordinate clause. The main clause gives us the most information and makes sense as a sentence on its own. Underline the main clause and circle the subordinate clause in each sentence below. One has been done for you.

1. (Although it was raining,) <u>the man went running</u>.
2. My Gran smokes, but only in her room.
3. If you pull the dog's tail, she will bite you.
4. My brother Tom likes to play cricket, but only at weekends.
5. Since you were last here we have made lots of changes to our house.

On the back of this sheet, write two simples sentences, two complex sentences and two compound sentences of your own.

Speech punctuation

When someone is actually speaking in a story it is called 'direct speech'. The words spoken have speech marks at the beginning and at the end.

'I am going to drink my beer,' said Gran.

If the writer tells the reader what someone has said, it is called 'reported speech'.

Gran said she was going to drink her beer.

Decide which of these is direct speech and add the speech marks and commas where appropriate.

1. *I'd like to do something different this year said Mum.*
2. *I thought what I'd really like to do is brew beer.*
3. *What do you two want to do? asked Gran.*
4. *Annie said she enjoyed the first aid course.*
5. *Dad said I want to learn how to do flower arranging.*
6. *Mum said she couldn't believe what Dad wanted to do.*

Rewrite the following passage, creating a new line each time a new person speaks. Don't forget the speech marks and commas!

Look everyone, I said I've got a brilliant idea! Calm down Sam, said Mum. You've knocked over the tomato sauce. Well, let's hear this wonderful idea snarled Annie, sarcastically. Give him a chance, Annie. It might be a really good idea said Gran puffing happily on her fag. As long as someone has an idea growled Dad. I'm fed up with sitting here.

_____

_____

_____

_____

_____

_____

_____

_____

Helpful hints for writing a family story

✦ A family story can be funny or sad. It can be about all sorts of families. The family might have a mum and dad, just one of these or someone else who looks after the children. The family can come from anywhere in the world. It can have any sort of lifestyle, such as being rich or poor or neither. They can be people who stay in one place or a family that travels. A family can have different sorts of family members. These can be grandparents, aunts and uncles, cousins and even family pets.

✦ A family story often has someone in the family who is unusual in some way. They may be a bit of a bully or they may be very adventurous or have an unusual hobby or ability. The story is often told by a member of the family who gets caught up in the actions of this unusual character.

✦ Sometimes the person telling the story can be a bit different, too. They don't have to be perfectly good and normal. The point of the family story is that a character or characters in the family creates havoc on the family in some way.

✦ When you are writing your story, try and make the things that happen exciting. Begin with describing the family in what is a normal situation for them and then allow the adventures to begin and perhaps get worse before ending the story in a happy way so that your readers feel that the family will be all right in the end.

✦ If you are going to write your story from the point of view of a family member, try to make your readers like the person telling the story. This way, whatever happens, the reader will be on the side of the person telling the story and will be more involved in the events and how it feels when these events occur.

✦ If you want your story to be funny, try to make the things that go wrong go really wrong. It won't be very funny if all that goes wrong is something simple that can easily be put right. Try to use your imagination and think of the most crazy thing you can. It is often funnier if a member of the family is different from what you would expect. For example, people expect mums to behave in a certain way, so make the mum in your story behave just as a mum wouldn't behave.

A family life story
Scaffold 1

You are going to write a family life story.
To help you plan your story, use the framework below.
Choose one option from each stage.

Stage One

Introduce the characters and set the scene.

A child lives with his/her parents. A relative is coming to stay for a holiday. The relative is:

a) a grandmother;

b) an uncle;

c) a grandad.

Stage Two

Give the characters a plan/a change/an adventure.

The visiting relative wants the child to help them with a new hobby. The new hobby is:

a) cooking;

b) magic tricks;

c) science experiments.

Stage Three

Start the characters off on their adventure.

The parents are going out. They leave the relative in charge of the child. The relative and the child get all the ingredients/equipment together in the kitchen to try out the new hobby. They plan a surprise for the parents because:

a) it is one of the parent's birthday;

b) it is their wedding anniversary;

c) the relative wants to say 'thank you' for letting him/her stay.

Stage Four

Give the characters a problem.

The relative and the child begin to cook/create tricks/do experiments. Things go wrong.

a) There is a huge explosion.

b) Something very strange is made.

c) The house is filled with smoke and a terrible smell.

WHICH PROBLEM SHALL I CHOOSE?

Stage Five

The problem is solved.

The parents return. They:

a) are very angry, but they clear up the mess;

b) they clear up the mess and decide to try the recipe/trick/experiment again, but properly;

c) clear up the mess and send the relative home.

Stage Six

Conclude the story.

After a few months, the family get a postcard from the relative.

Wish you were here!

a) The relative is staying with someone else and is going to try their hobby again, much to the alarm of the family.

b) The visitor has joined evening classes to learn how to do their hobby properly.

c) The visitor has decided on another hobby – making fireworks.

A family life story
Vocabulary bank 1

acrid
amazing
angry

blasting
bungalow
bunson burner

calamity
cloak
conjuring
cottage
cough

demolish
dense

elderly
erupting
excitement
experiment
explosion

fantastic
flat

hobby

ingredients

magic words

outrage

pastime
peculiar
powders

rabbits
recipe
relative

semi-detached
special
spells

vacation
visit

wizened

My own words

A family life story
Scaffold 2

You are going to write a family life story.
To help you plan your story, use the framework below.
Choose one option from each stage.

Stage One

Introduce the characters and set the scene.

There is a family who live in an ordinary house. They are:

a) a mum, dad and two boys;

b) a mum, dad and two girls;

c) a mum, dad and one boy and one girl.

Stage Two

Give the characters a plan/a change/an adventure

The family have been chosen for a television programme.
They are going to be filmed living in a rainforest to see how
well they survive together. They are allowed to take:

a) medicines;

b) books;

c) cooking equipment.

Stage Three

Start the characters off on their adventure.

In the jungle:

a) Dad decides he is the survival expert;

b) Mum decides she is the survival expert;

c) one of the children decide they are the survival expert;

d) they all decide they are the survival experts.

The survival expert(s) catches snakes for the others to eat, chops down trees on top of the
camp, covers everyone with mud while they are asleep to stop the flies biting them, makes
clothes out of leaves for the others to wear.

Stage Four

Give the characters a problem.

After many rainy days, there is no food. The survival expert(s) makes the others hunt for food. They travel miles through muddy, hot, tangled jungle. They:

a) fish in a crocodile infested river. An angry crocodile is about to attack them.

b) join a pack of gorillas to share their food. The big, chief, male gorilla is very angry and is about to attack them.

c) make a camp fire and fall asleep. When they wake up they are surrounded by hungry wild animals.

Stage Five

The problem is solved.

a) The television camera crew rescue them.

b) The television company has received so many complaints from the viewing public about the danger the family are in that they decide to rescue them.

c) One of the family appears to go mad and jumps around singing and dancing. This astonishes the animal(s) so much it/they stop in their tracks. The family run for their lives and escape.

Stage Six

Conclude the story.

a) The family are famous. The survival expert(s) has/have a new role advising others on surviving in the jungle.

b) The family return home and decide that the nearest they will ever get to wild animals is at a zoo.

c) The family return home. The television company asks them to do a new programme on surviving in the desert. They begin to pack.

A family life story
Vocabulary bank 2

advisory capacity	glinting	rainforest
aggravating	homeopathic	relief
	humidity	remote
boom		
	insanity	slithery
camera	inundated	sound
crew	irritating	steaming
		survival
daggers	lurking	
demolish		teeth like
	massive	television
encyclopaedia		torrential
engineer	not too friendly	
everyday	nuisance	unexceptional
expert		utensils
	panic	
ferocious	poisonous	
	programme	

My own words

Daring Derek

'Hello, Derek!' said a steamy voice.

I opened one eye slowly and sure enough there was the dragon.

'That was quick, Singe.' I exclaimed in surprise. 'I'd only just dozed off.'

Singe never turned up in the normal places that you'd expect to find dragons, like behind the sofa or in the shadowy cupboard under the stairs. No, he always snuck up on me, just as I snuggled into my feathery duvet and fell asleep. He was the smartest dragon; covered in red metallic scales with a spiky tail that lounged across the bedroom floor. He was so heavy that when he jumped on my bed, we both rolled into the centre of the mattress. I could feel him radiating heat like a giant hot-water bottle. He had the smelliest dragon breath of all, so I usually turfed him out of bed and made him sit on my beanbag.

Now, you may be wondering why I didn't scream for help. Well, parents aren't much of a match for a dragon that has just dropped in to visit. They'd simply call out the police or the army and then I'd just have to explain how the dragon got here, and you know adults never believe anything that you tell them! But I'll let you in on the secret.

I created him in my mind. I made Singe to be my imaginary friend and now he exists in THE WORLD OF IMAGINATION and can appear when he wants to. It's simple really; anyone can do it. You know when you are in bed, feeling very relaxed but you haven't quite dropped off to sleep? Well, that's the DOZING ZONE. Anything is possible in the DOZING ZONE. It's where you can tap into your mind's eye and generate anything that you want to. Of course you can exercise your imagination at other times too.

You know how your teacher is always nagging you to use your imagination and write more interesting stories? Then just when you have thought of something pretty amazing, she tells you to stop daydreaming and get your maths book out? Well, daydreaming is like a door to THE WORLD OF IMAGINATION that you can never quite open properly. No sooner have you squeezed your foot through the gap than you are dragged back to reality. Now we really ought to turn our attention to Singe because he is riding my skateboard around the room and blowing sparks at the soccer hero posters on the walls.

'We have to go,' whispered Singe, sounding just like a piece of paper crackling as it catches fire. 'There is an urgent situation in THE WORLD OF IMAGINATION and you have been summoned to an Emergency Meeting. Hurry up or we'll be late.'

Well, you don't argue with a dragon do you? I climbed onto his neck, grabbed his knotty horns and clung on like a limpet.

'Hang on tight!' he shouted, spitting shiny embers into the air. Next minute we dived through a hole in the floor because he was too large to fit through the window.

Have you ever ridden a dragon? I always find that Singes's smoke blows into my eyes and makes them sting. The hole in the floor was full of pulsating coloured lights that squeaked as we flew past. I was beginning to feel rather queasy, when the coloured lights disappeared and we ground to a sudden halt.

'Here we are!' wheezed Singed who was completely out of puff after flying so fast. 'Off you get.'

I have often visited THE WORLD OF IMAGINATION and there is one aspect of being there that I particularly enjoy. You see, in THE REAL WORLD I am a weedy nine-year-old boy with arms and legs like sticks of celery. The most muscled parts of my legs are my knobbly knee caps; even my grandma makes jokes about my scrawny chicken legs! However, as soon as I set foot in this imaginary world, I have the body of a World Wrestling Federation champion and the strength to tackle anything! It's all very cool!

The most amazing spectacle met my eyes. Congregated in front of a semicircular stage was a huge crowd. There were colossal giants and bearded dwarves, flickering fairies and warty witches, beautiful heroines and handsome princes all twittering away like a flock of worried sparrows. I turned to Singe who was chatting excitedly to a small white unicorn.

'Excuse me! What is going on?' I demanded. 'Where did all these…?'

'Shh!' whispered the unicorn. 'The meeting has begun.'

There was a strange humming in the air, a crackling sensation that made my hair stand on end and then a vivid streak of electric-blue lightning struck the platform in a shower of fiery sparks. Singe grunted in approval at this display. 'It always knows how to make a grand entrance,' he said as a robed figure stepped out of the smoke.

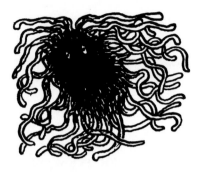

'Thank you all for coming to this important meeting,' it said in an unknown language that everyone in the audience could understand. 'WE HAVE A SERIOUS PROBLEM! Some child, somewhere in THE REAL WORLD, has a very good imagination! They have obviously been watching the 'Creatures of the deep' programme on the Discovery Channel and then looking at the stars through their telescope before they go to bed. The end result of all this is a bad dream about an evil Black-Hole-Jellyfish that wants to eat everything in the Universe. That jellyfish, being the result of intense thought processes, has now turned up in our WORLD with the sole aim of sucking us all into its core of nothingness.'

At this point, the audience became very agitated. The robed figure on the dais threw down another lightning bolt to restore order and continued to address the crowd.

'In an attempt to destroy the evil Black-Hole-Jellyfish – which in addition to being rather mean, is absolutely huge – I deployed some of our most powerful forces but to no avail.' The robed figure swept his arm across the stage and a trio of depressed-looking wizards could be seen, whittling away at gnarled tree branches with Swiss army knives.

'The Three Mages tried to subdue the creature with mighty magic but it sucked their wands right out of their hands and left them as defenceless as newborn babies.' A horrified gasp went up from the audience.

'Our most noble and gargantuan giant rescued the helpless wizards.' A cheer went up from the crowd as an embarrassed giant in a large red blanket, appeared on the stage next to the wand-making wizards.

'He made a great effort to roll up the evil Black-Hole-Jellyfish; to make it suck itself to nothing. However, this plan failed when his clothes were dragged into the black hole, leaving him in his birthday suit. No one in their right mind would face a Black-Hole-Jellyfish in this state and he wisely withdrew from the area. A new outfit of breeches and jerkin is at this very moment being stitched together by the nimble-fingered elves and we trust that the brave giant will be feeling better soon!'

The giant went an even brighter shade of crimson and hid his head under the blanket. The audience all applauded loudly and looked expectantly at the robed figure on the stage.

'I was left with only one option. I sent Singe the dragon to bring Daring Derek to our WORLD.'

'Daring Derek, you are the only one with the strength to contain the Black-Hole-Jellyfish. You must collect THE ROCKS THAT WON'T BUDGE from around THE WORLD OF IMAGINATION and use them to enclose the creature.'

I was a feeling rather anxious at this point in time. I knew about THE ROCKS THAT WON'T BUDGE! They were large grumpy boulders that would just turn up where you least wanted them and then, despite all protests, they would refuse to move until it suited them. Even with my tuned wrestler body they could prove rather a handful, let alone using them to trap a mean-spirited Black-Hole-Jellyfish!

'Singe the dragon will assist you of course,' added the robed figure helpfully. 'The safety of our WORLD is in your hands. Good luck.' With that there was another bolt of blue lightning and the thing in the robe disappeared.

The rest of the crowd were keen to do their part and sent out search parties to locate any of THE ROCKS THAT WON'T BUDGE that were in the area. I climbed aboard the dragon again and we circled overhead to see the exact location of the Black-Hole-Jellyfish. It wasn't hard to make out. There was an ever-increasing tide of emptiness around it; the closest things were drawn into its pitch-black depths.

I have to say that THE ROCKS THAT WON'T BUDGE were less of a problem than you might imagine. Most folk when they find a huge boulder blocking their door or path, will either make a futile attempt to push it out of the way or clamber over. This just serves to make THE ROCKS THAT WON'T BUDGE angry and they remain where they are. The secret to relocating them requires very little in the way of upper body strength: they just like to be tickled!

After a couple of hours of tickling, we had enough rocks to surround the murky sinkhole that was the Black-Hole-Jellyfish. The pull of the black hole helped a great deal by dragging the boulders towards itself. At the same time Singe was using his wings as bellows, firing up his internal inferno chamber. When he had built up enough pressure and THE ROCKS THAT WON'T BUDGE were just about to be consumed by the Black-Hole-Jellyfish force field, Singe expelled a huge burst of white-hot flame. The heat of his fire liquefied the rocks, which, as they reformed, created an immovable bunker around the jellyfish, sealing it inside. The deed was done!

As if by magic, the crowd of imaginary creatures appeared again and a wild party began. Singe and I were heroes; the wizards waved their freshly whittled wands and the giant looked very dashing in his new outfit. Even the robed figure patted me on the back.

Yawning, I realised how tired I was and asked Singe to take me home. Even a hero needs his sleep, especially when he is going to wake up the next day with scrawny chicken legs!

Understanding the grammar and punctuation

Adjectives

Adjectives are describing words.

They describe nouns (people, places, things).

a _steamy,_ voice, _normal_ places, _knobbly_ knees.

Adjectival phrases

You can use several adjectives to describe a single noun.

A _vivid streak of electric blue lightning_ struck the platform.

Singe expelled a _huge burst of white-hot flame._

Comparative and superlative adjectives

You use these adjectives to describe likenesses and differences.

Comparative adjectives compare two things.

The suffix 'er' is added to the adjective to show more or less.

The blue dragon was warm but the yellow dragon was warmer.

The troll was heavier than the dwarf.

The dwarf was shorter than the troll.

Superlative adjectives describe the most or least.

The red dragon was the warmest.

The giant was the heaviest of all.

Apostrophes for contractions

A contraction is two words shortened into one.

An apostrophe is used where the letters have been dropped.

I have – I've; did not – didn't; we will – we'll; he is – he's

Adjectives

Read this paragraph. Underline the adjectives.

Congregated in front of a semi-circular stage was a huge crowd. There were colossal giants and bearded dwarves, flickering fairies and warty witches, beautiful heroines and handsome princes, all twittering away like a flock of worried sparrows.

Complete this adjective grid.

1. _____	_____*bigger*_____	_____
2. ____*small*____	_____	____*smallest*____
3. _____	_____*scarier*_____	_____
4. ____*bright*____	_____	_____
5. _____	____*grumpier*____	_____
6. _____	_____	_____*bravest*_____

Rewrite these sentences using comparative and superlative adjectives.

1. *The goblin was more ugly than the dwarf but the troll was the most ugly of all.*

_____

_____

2. *Daring Derek was more happy than he had ever been before.*

_____

3. *The wizard was made even more angry by the witch's cheeky cat.*

_____

On the back of this sheet, use adjectival phrases to write your own description of a dragon.

Apostrophes and contractions

Rewrite each sentence, replacing the underlined words with the correct contraction from the box.

didn't   aren't   what's   you've

1. Parents <u>are not</u> much of a match for a dragon like Singe.

   _____

2. <u>You have</u> been summoned to an emergency meeting.

   _____

3. '<u>What is</u> going on?' I demanded. 'Where did all these...?'

   _____

4. Now, you may be wondering why I <u>did not</u> scream for help?

   _____

Contractions

Write the two words that form each of these contractions.

1. He'll   _____   _____

2. Should've   _____   _____

3. We're   _____   _____

4. Can't   _____   _____

5. Don't   _____   _____

Write the two words that have been contracted to make **won't**.

   _____   _____

Helpful hints for writing a fantasy story

✦ Fantasy stories usually include mysterious worlds, magical creatures and strange happenings. For example:

Daring Derek met giants, dragons, wizards, unicorns, witches and fairies!

✦ Your story settings are very important because they affect how your characters feel and behave. Use lots of interesting adjectives to describe the scene and the characters.

✦ Describe the differences between the real world and your fantasy setting. This will help the reader to be drawn into the story.

✦ Work out how your characters are going to pass from one world to the next. You could give magical powers to everyday items – make a bed or carpet fly, for example. Another way of reaching the other world is through magical entrances such as doors or mirrors.

✦ Give your characters special powers when they pass into the fantasy world. Scrawny Derek became Daring Derek the super strong hero!

✦ Your main characters should play an important part in helping to solve a problem in the other world. You will need to decide upon the challenge they face and then show how they overcome it.

✦ In fantasy stories, time can pass at different rates in the various worlds.

✦ You will need to work out how you are going to return your characters to their own world.

✦ Another feature of fantasy stories is that the characters are often changed for the better by their adventures.

✦ If you wish your character to be able to return to the other world for more adventures, you will need to make sure that the openings between the worlds are kept open at the end of your story. This leaves the reader with the hint of more fantastic stories to come!

Fantasy story
Scaffold 1

You are going to write a fantasy story.
To help plan your story, use the framework below.
Choose one option from each stage.

Stage One

Choose the characters for your story.

a) A boy and a fiery dragon.

b) A boy and a shimmering unicorn.

Stage Two

Start your story with a good beginning.

a) He had just finished reading his book and turned to switch off the light. A movement caught his eye and he realised that he was not alone. Standing in the shadows was a ...

b) He just couldn't sleep! He tossed and turned for ages. Suddenly a bright light appeared near his bed and there before his eyes was a ...

Stage Three

Set the scene for the story.

The unusual visitor explained that it came from a magical world and that they needed his help. The boy agreed to go with it at once because:

a) he was promised special powers;

b) he was feeling brave and it said he was the only one who could save their world.

As they travelled into the magical world, his new friend explained the danger he would have to face.

Stage Four

Give the characters a problem.

A black hole had appeared in the ground and was sucking everything into its centre. No one had been able to stop it and they were afraid that their whole world would be destroyed, The boy realised that:

a) he now had magical powers and could make things change shape;

b) he had the ability to hear what the black hole was saying.

The black hole told him that it always felt empty, so it kept on pulling things towards itself. It was also very lonely because everyone was scared of it.

Stage Five

Say how the problem is solved.

With the help of his friend, the boy used his magical powers to transform the black hole into a:

HOW SHALL I SOLVE THE PROBLEM?

a) a large black talking rock that could move around;

b) a black talking hat that he gave to his friend to keep him company.

The black hole was no longer a threat. The boy was a hero!

Stage Six

Say how the story ends.

The window between the two worlds was difficult to find again. The boy was tempted to stay longer and explore but he realised that he did not know how much time had passed at home.

a) He had to return to his own world but his new friends promised that they would guard the opening between the two worlds so that he could visit again.

b) He arrived back in his own room just as his mother came in to see if he was asleep.

Fantasy story
Vocabulary bank 1

amazing	help, assist	real
astonishing	heroes, heroines	red, scarlet
big, bigger, biggest	imagine, imagination	scales
boulder, rock, stone		secret
brave	knobbly, knotty	sleep, tired, yawn
		smellier, smelliest
celebrate	large, larger, largest	spiky
creatures		strange, weird
	magic	
daring	mean, nasty, evil	time
deed	metallic, tinny	trap, capture
door	mirror	troll
dragon		
dwarf, dwarves	noise	urgent
fairy, fairies	opening	visit
fire, sparks		
	prince, princess	witch
giant, ogre	problem	wizard
		wonderful
		world

My own words

Fantasy story
Scaffold 2

You are going to write a fantasy story.
To help plan your story, use the framework below.
Choose one option from each stage.

Stage One

Choose the characters for your story.

a) Two best friends who were building a tree house at the end of the garden.

b) Identical twins who were always arguing. They were sent outside to get some fresh air because they were annoying their mother.

Stage Two

Start your story with a good beginning.

a) A rope ladder hung creaking from the gnarled oak tree – it was strange that they had never noticed it before. It was too tempting to resist and they both scrambled up.

b) Pushing and shoving the children fought over who should go down the slide first. Still scrapping, they slid simultaneously down the slide.

They never reached the end. There was a strange noise and they felt themselves suddenly being yanked / catapulted / drawn by an invisible force. Describe the sensation.

Stage Three

Set the scene for the story.

All was still. They stared in disbelief at the sight before their eyes.

a) They were in a land where everything was ice. Strange ice creatures approached them saying that they needed help to stop their world thawing.

b) They were in a castle chamber surrounded by unusual creatures. They were told that they had been summoned to rescue the queen, who had been kidnapped by an evil goblin / troll / giant.

Stage Four

Give the characters a problem.

The children were given a magical potion to drink. It gave them special powers so that they could fly/become invisible/had superhuman strength/hypnotise things.

a) They had to find the Ice Crystal that had been stolen by the Mud Men. The Mud King wanted the ice to melt, so that the world would turn to mud and he would be in control.

b) The Queen was a prisoner in a great fortified tower and nobody had been able to rescue her.

The children would only be able to return home once they had completed the task.

Stage Five

The problem is solved.

The children have to combine their special powers to fulfil their difficult tasks. They will be able to return home once they have completed the mission they have been charged with.

a) They managed to steal back the Ice Crystal from the Mud King's swamp but one of them was badly injured in the attempt.

b) They managed to foil all the tower's booby-traps and outwit the evil goblin/troll/giant but one of them was badly injured in the attempt.

Stage Six

Say how the story ends.

The injured child was healed by magic. The celebrated heroes lost their special powers but were given gifts in return:

a) a magic crystal that will let them see what is going on in the Ice Kingdom;

b) a mirror that will let them see what is happening in the other world.

When they returned to the real world they find that no time has passed at all. They promised to keep their adventure a secret. (Who would believe them anyway?)

Fantasy story
Vocabulary bank 2

bewitched

capture
castle, citadel
catapulted
celebrated
chamber
child, children
chilling
clambered
creature
crystal

defrost
determined
disbelief
dwarf

enchantment
extraordinary

fortress

giant, ogre

goblin

heal, healed
hero, heroine

identical twin
injury

magic, magical
manage, managed
mission

outwit

plight
promise

quagmire

real world
rescue
return

seize

sensation, feeling
special
spell
strange
strength
summoned
super-human
swamp, bog

task, burden, labour
thaw
tower
troll
turret

unusual

vow

weird
wounded

yanked, pulled

My own words

The Space Travellers

'RISE AND SHINE!' beeped the droid as it smoothly drew back the solar shields. 'Did the asteroid shower keep you awake?'

'No, I slept like a dead star,' yawned Serena. 'Are the others up yet?'

'Yes. I believe you are – technically speaking – late!' grimaced the droid. 'For your information the year is 2090; we are cruising at warp three and the outside temperature is...'

Interrupting with an uncomplimentary comment about the time-keeping properties of certain robot types, Serena slipped into her uniform. She jumped into her travel pod and zoomed through the habitation quarters like a comet. As she approached the Astroschool Deck she hovered like a hawk, so that the door droid could identify her retinal scan.

'ENTER.'

'I'm glad I'm not the last into class,' someone gasped behind her.

'Hi, Jez. Did you forget to put your pod on charge again last night?'

'Very funny!'

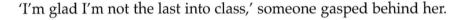

The Astroschool Deck comprised rows of high-tech chairs with humming computer monitors. All but two of the chairs were occupied by children; they in turn were kept fully occupied by the Hologram Tutor who was running through the day's timetable. Serena and Jez slipped as unobtrusively as possible into their seats and donned their brainwave helmets. They were aware of how vital it was that they didn't miss anything.

The Hologram Tutor moved onto its favourite speech about how the whole mission had come to pass. The students knew it all off by heart but that didn't prevent the shimmering hologram from going through it all again – yet again!

'All you children have been specially selected for this crucial space mission. The Earth, our home planet, is becoming overpopulated and natural resources are rapidly being used up. Many attempts have been made to colonise other planets in our solar system but all have failed. In a last desperate bid to save the world, scientists sent an SOS message into space, hardly believing that they would get a response.

'To everyone's surprise we received a reply from a distant solar system that had several uninhabited planets. It seemed that the local aliens thought that one of these would suit us Earthlings. They sent detailed plans for a strange spaceship via radio signals that we picked up and decoded with the huge satellite dishes that scan the deepness of space. Earth scientists pooled their knowledge and skills and this weird craft is the result.'

The children heaved a communal sigh of relief thinking that the Hologram Tutor had finished but...

'Unfortunately, the new planetary system is too far away for adults to travel there, since they would have died of old age before they arrived. Therefore it is you, children, who have been given the task of setting up the new planet. As you voyage boldly through the vast expanse of nothing that is space, you will learn all the necessary skills to set up the new planet for its future inhabitation by Earth creatures, assisted of course by the multifunctional droids that accompany you.'

There was a pause... and hopeful glances all around...

'In order to achieve this great feat and ultimately ensure the continuation of Earthly species you children have been enhanced. You are lucky enough to have had sophisticated memory chips that give you the ability to recall huge amounts of data inserted into your brains. (Not as much as my data banks, I might add, but no computer expects humans to be perfect!) The people on Earth have pinned all their hopes for survival on you brave children. They do not intend all the pollution and destruction that have been a part of Earth's history to travel with you to the new planet. Therefore you will pay attention to your lessons!'

The students shifted restlessly in their chairs. Long monologues like this always made their memory chips itch. Despite living with this great responsibility, they were just like ordinary children. They liked pop music, computer games – and leaving their clothes all over the floor (this is where the droids came into their own, they never got tired of clearing up the spacecraft!).

The children were able to keep in touch with their families through their virtual reality cabins, so they didn't get homesick. They also had examples of most of the flora and fauna from Earth, living in special microclimates all over the spacecraft. It was rather like a flying planet in its own right.

'Today you will be learning about some of the aliens who inhabit the neighbouring planets. Please do not be alarmed by the appearance of some of them. We are going to have to learn to live together despite our very obvious differences.'

All at once, the Hologram Tutor's image flickered in the air and disappeared with a brief 'POP'! In the next instant, the spacecraft was rocked by a huge blast: the battle alarm sounded throughout the ship and the children ran to their emergency stations.

'WE ARE CURRENTLY UNDER ATTACK FROM A ZOLIN PIRATE SPACE CRUISER. THEY INSIST THAT WE SURRENDER,' reported the communications droid. 'HOW SHALL I RESPOND?'

'Let's see if they understand this!'

From their positions on the flight deck, Serena and Jez operated their laser blasters. They fired repeatedly on the unidentified craft that was trying to capture their ship. Another explosion rocked the control centre and Jez was catapulted from his safety harness to lie motionless on the floor.

Serena had no time to see if he was alive – she donned her virtual fighting visor. This was a prototype weapon that should allow her to infiltrate the Zolin computer banks and disable their firing systems, thereby making them helpless. However, it was a high risk, untested weapon and Serena's memory chip might blow a circuit and kill her.

'I haven't travelled all these light years to miss seeing my new planet!' she yelled at the Zolins, activating her visor.

Time seemed to stand still. A medic droid hovered above Jez. Serena sat motionless. All firing ceased. Then, WHOOSH! The Zolin ship exploded.

The aftershock made Jez groan as he regained consciousness. Serena removed her visor with shaking hands. The communication droid let out a metallic cheer.

'I have reset the coordinates for our new planet,' it burbled. 'Warp four, all systems are go! Estimated time of arrival six hours. The temperature outside is...'

Understanding the grammar and punctuation

Word order in sentences

All sentences contain a subject and a verb.

Usually the subject of the sentence comes in front of the verb.

The spacecraft was *rocked* by a huge blast.

    subject   verb

If we change the order of the words, the sentence may lose its original meaning or make no sense at all.

A huge blast was rocked by the spacecraft.

Some adverbs can be moved within a sentence without changing its meaning.

'RISE AND SHINE!' beeped the droid as it smoothly drew back the solar shields.

'RISE AND SHINE!' beeped the droid as it drew back the solar shields smoothly.

Apostrophe for possession

An apostrophe (') can be used to show belonging or possession.

the Earth's history

means

the history of the Earth

When there is more than one owner, place the apostrophe after the plural owner.

the ships of the Zolins

becomes

the Zolins' ships

Name

Changing the order of words in a sentence

1. Choose words from the list below to create a sentence.

   the alien   the robot   the planet   the spaceship
   around   flew   and

   _____

2. Rewrite your sentence with a different word order so that it keeps its original meaning.

   _____

3. Now change the word order so that it no longer makes sense.

   _____

Rewrite these sentences so that the position of the adverb is changed but the meaning of the sentence remains the same.

1. *The astronaut <u>rapidly</u> put on her spacesuit.*

   _____

2. *<u>Surprisingly</u>, the meteor shower did little damage to the rocket.*

   _____

3. *The alien waved its tentacles <u>wildly</u> at the robot.*

   _____

4. *The robots <u>hurriedly</u> repaired the ship's deflector shields.*

   _____

5. *<u>Silently</u>, the UFO skimmed the surface of the red planet.*

   _____

6. *The craters on the asteroid <u>continuously</u> blew out poisonous gases into the atmosphere.*

   _____

Name

Apostrophe of possession

Rewrite these phrases to show an apostrophe of possession. For example:

the uniform of the captain   *the captain's uniform*

1. *the ship of the alien* _____

2. *the surface of the planet* _____

3. *the engine of the rocket* _____

4. *the light of the star* _____

5. *the weapon of the aliens* _____

6. *the orbits of the planets* _____

7. *the spacesuits of the astronauts* _____

8. *the direction of the asteroids* _____

Insert apostrophes into these sentences to show possession

1. *The aliens head was poking up over the craters edge.*

2. *The UFOs doors opened to reveal the robots control pods.*

3. *The ships captain was in charge of the childrens safety.*

4. *The suns rays melted all of the mens spacesuits.*

5. *The telescopes images helped the astronauts to plot the spaceships route.*

There is a mistake in the use of one of the apostrophes in this sentence. Circle the error and write a sentence explaining why it is wrong.

The robots' metal feet made the spaceship's hull shake, as they chased the angry alien invader back into it's pod.

Helpful hints for writing a science fiction story.

✦ Science fiction writing can be serious in tone, sometimes even frightening.

✦ You might choose to set your science fiction story in a future world, or against the backdrop of an unknown planet. Or you might place your characters in the modern world, but threaten them with alien invasion.

✦ Your story should include some ordinary characters with whom the reader can identify. The contrast between these characters and the extraordinary nature of the challenges they face will therefore have more impact.

✦ If you include aliens in your story, be careful when you describe them. If you make their appearance too way-out it might make them seem comic rather than frightening.

✦ When the characters address one another, they may well refer to some sort of futuristic gadgets.

✦ You should include some of the following science fiction ideas in your story:

time travel; space travel; encounters with alien life-forms; the threat of world domination by hostile alien invaders; and advanced machine-dependent people.

✦ Show the problems faced by people living in the future, or on other planets, and how these problems throw light on, or serve as a warning about, aspects of life on our planet today.

✦ Use some techniques to create suspense.

✦ Include descriptions of forms of transport, clothing, food and weapons in future worlds.

✦ In science fiction adventures, the characters usually overcome the difficulties they face.

Science fiction story
Scaffold 1

You are going to write a science fiction story.
To help plan your story, use the framework below.
Choose one option from each stage.

Stage One

Choose the characters for your story.

a) Two children who are in the school Stargazer's Club
   and are desperate to meet an alien.

b) A brother and sister whose astronaut parents saw
   aliens and their spaceship on one of their journeys into
   space.

Stage Two

Start your story with a good beginning.

'Do you suppose anyone else saw it? We can't be the only ones! Wow! This could be really
big news.'

a) The characters witness an amazing meteor shower, right over their school.

b) The characters notice an unusual green fog hovering over their town.

Stage Three

Set the scene for the story.

Things are not right at school! All the teachers seem to be acting
very oddly. They are looking at the children in strange ways.

a) Their class teacher says they have a new project called
   'Earthlings'. The whole class has to be weighed, measured,
   x-rayed, have hair samples taken and their teeth counted.

b) The children are given a collection of strange metallic objects
   and a diagram. They were told they had to assemble the objects
   according to the diagram.

Stage Four

Give the characters a problem.

The characters realise that something is very wrong. They spy on the teachers while they are in the staffroom and discover that aliens have possessed the teachers' bodies.

a) The aliens had planned to study the children in order to find out enough about humans to take over the Earth.

b) The aliens' spaceship had been damaged and they had had to make an emergency landing on Earth. They did not want to be discovered while making repairs so they had possessed the teachers' bodies and found a way to get the children to help them mend their spaceship.

Stage Five

Say how the problem is solved.

The aliens leave the teachers' bodies, capture the two characters and take them to their spaceship.

a) The characters are made to describe all the problems that Earthlings are faced with. The aliens decide that they do not want to get involved with such primitive life forms. They get ready to leave immediately.

b) The characters are considered too small to be a threat to the aliens. They get to see all over the spaceship. The Earth's gravity begins to make the aliens sick so they have to leave.

Stage Six

Say how the story ends.

The characters are bursting to tell people about their adventure but they know that no-one will believe their story. Instead...

a) They write an article for a space magazine and win a prize – a trip to orbit Earth in a rocket.

b) They take the test to become astronauts and pass with full marks. They become the youngest astronauts in space and meet some more aliens!

Science fiction story
Vocabulary bank 1

asteroid shower
astronaut
alien
atmosphere

believe
brightness

colonise
comet

damage
decision
defend, defence

Earthling
emergency landing
examination
extraterrestrial

flash
floating

gleaming

human

inhabit
instruments
invade
investigate

launch
lift-off

metallic
meteor

observation
orbit
oxygen

planet, galaxy

repair
robot
rocket

space
spacecraft, spaceship
space traveller
suspicious

telescope
training

UFO
understand
universe
unusual, strange

weapon
weightlessness

My own words

Science fiction story
Scaffold 2

You are going to write a science fiction story.
To help plan your story, use the framework below.
Choose one option from each stage.

Stage One

Choose the characters for your story.

a) A family on a stargazing outing. There had been several
reports of UFO sightings in the area and they were keen to
try and spot one.

b) A young astronomers' group outing to an observatory. They
run a website about the night sky and needed new footage
for their video clips.

Stage Two

Start your story with a good beginning.

a) The night was dark with not a cloud in the sky. The conditions were perfect for stargazing.
The telescopes were polished and focused. It was the large UFO hovering above them that
was the problem.

b) First came the light, a blinding flash that hurt their eyes, then a massive booming sound
that threw them to the ground. The spaceship had landed.

Stage Three

Set the scene for the story.

It was like nothing that they had ever seen before.

a) The characters were powerless against a suction
beam that dragged them into the hull of the
spacecraft.

b) Small space pods emerged from the Mother Ship and
rounded up the humans, forcing them into the
spacecraft.

Stage Four

Give the characters a problem.

a) The aliens were collecting specimens for their intergalactic zoo and the humans were to be the newest attractions.

b) The aliens wanted to conduct experiments on humans to collect data about their bodies and the way they live.

Stage Five

Say how the problem is solved.

They were able to communicate using mind-reading helmets that project images onto a screen. They did not want to hurt humans, just find out more about this weird species.

a) In order to be able to stay on Earth, the humans agreed to wear tracking devices so that the aliens could observe their activities from their home planet.

b) One person volunteered to go with the aliens to their planet, so that the other humans could stay on Earth.

Stage Six

Say how the story ends.

The humans were released safely.

a) The whole event was wiped from the characters' memory banks. They did not know it but the aliens were still monitoring them.

b) No one believed the characters' story; they thought it was a practical joke. The unexplained disappearance of one of the group remained a mystery.

Science Fiction
Scaffold 2

alien	fiery	persuade
astronomy	flash, streak	probe
beam of light	galaxy	satellite
bright		shooting star
	halt, stop	sighting
capsule, pod	helmet	signal
capture		spacecraft
chase	implant	spaceship
comet	intergalactic	specimen
communicate		
cosmos	lens	telepathy
	life form	telescope
deactivate		tracking device
drawn up, sucked up	meteor	
		UFO (Unidentified Flying Object)
experiment	observatory	

My own words

The scrapbook

The night was dark. The candles flickered. The house was old … and it was listening.

'I just happen to find electricity quite useful, that's all! It doesn't mean that I don't like it here!'

'The house is decrepit, the wiring is faulty and the electrician seems to have gone missing.' His mother rolled her eyes in exasperation. 'Just what am I supposed to do about it?'

'I don't think that the house wants us here. It doesn't want to be changed.'

'Nonsense, this place will be fantastic once we have renovated it!' With that happy thought, she trod a careful path through the rotten timbers of the hall floor and was swallowed up by the gloom of the kitchen.

Tom sighed. Oh yeh. This house was a real bargain! Only his parents would buy a property where the previous owner had disappeared under mysterious circumstances and every room was in a dilapidated state – except for the library. The library was weird. He always felt as if it was the heart of the house; the chamber that pumped life into the rickety walls and kept the whole place standing. Groaning shelves lined it from floor to ceiling, looking as if they were about to buckle under the weight of the leather bound books. Wooden shutters over the windows prevented the sunlight from getting in and heavy dust aged in the air. The books themselves seemed to beg to be released from the shelves. There were some very unusual titles with bizarre illustrations and Tom could lose himself for hours in their pages.

There was one book in particular that had come to his attention. It had a blood-red cover and the pattern up the spine looked like grasping fingers. The book was entitled, 'My Life' but there was no mention of an author and the pages were blank. Tom decided to use it as a scrapbook and immediately scrawled his name on the front page.

In the days that followed, Tom added photographs and mementos of his life to the book. Pictures of him and his school friends at his last party, the newspaper clipping of when he won a skateboarding competition and the ticket from his trip on the London Eye. He even managed to get a paw print from his dog, Scruffy, by leaving the book open on the floor just inside the front door. The pages were filling up.

Things were not going well with the house. Every time an area was worked on, it revealed more that needed fixing. It was as if the house were rotten on the inside. The peeling plaster and rotten boards were merely the oozing scabs on a far deeper wound. Workmen arrived and then left with excuses and tasks unfinished. Money was tight. Tempers were frayed.

The school holidays came round and Tom tried hard to ease the burden on his parents. He wrenched up loose timbers and scraped at the grungy old paper that clung to the resistant walls. Blisters grew and burst on his fingers as he wrestled with piles of rubble, his torn and jagged fingernails a sign of his struggles. He began to view the house as a giant onion with layer upon layer of putrid skin that needed to be peeled away.

In the midst of all this work, Tom was secreting parts of his life in the welcoming pages of the book. Every item seemed to fit into its own place on the page, like a piece in a favourite jigsaw. When he came to the double spread at the heart of the book he began to map out his family tree. In no time at all, the images of his parents smiled out from the paper. His little sister, who had died when only a few days old, was there in the single picture of her that he owned. The grandparents he had never met watched him gravely and even Scruffy had been immortalised in a print. He was now more than half way through the book – his life.

The house was putting up a fight. It was as if it did not want to be altered. Tom's father was injured when a ceiling collapsed and his mother had to give up work to look after him. Time passed. Costs rose. Anxiety spread. Money was tight. Tempers were short.

The family spent more and more of their time in the house. Tom spent most of his time in the library. It was the only room in the house that had not been touched; the shelves continued to battle against the downward force of the books, the light was still barred from entering. However, Tom's interest in other books had faded. He felt that he had to fill up the remaining few empty leaves in his own book, that this was all that mattered. He began to include drawings of his own; drawings of the house. They were all in charcoal: black shadows with smudged lines. That was how he was beginning to feel, as if he were smudged around the edges. The house was beating him: it was beating them all.

There came the day that Tom turned to the last page. He could hear his parents arguing in the kitchen. Scruffy was nowhere to be found but there was a lot of his fur on the library floor. The book felt heavy in his hands: it bulged with the details of his life and there was only one page left. He wondered how to fill that final space. He had no more photographs to stick in. Everyone he knew and cared about was already between the pages.

He decided to sketch a picture of himself, a self-portrait. As his hand moved across the paper, the charcoal lines began to take shape. His head, his features looked back at him as he filled in his own details…his reflection stared out at him. No longer

was he able to hear his parents' voices, the house was silent. It was strange, he thought, all that work and the house appeared exactly the same – still rotten. Now he had drawn his hands, his legs, his feet. Why were his parents so quiet? His picture was finished. There he was on the page. In the bottom corner he wrote, 'This is Me. This is my life.' And then as an afterthought, 'The End!'

A few days later the police arrived. None of the family had been seen for a while and a neighbour had reported that the windows and doors were all wide open. The house was deserted. All traces of Tom and his parents were gone. The police searched the house from top to bottom but there was no sign of life. An official investigation was set up but it provided no answers.

Months passed and a 'For Sale' sign was erected in the house's overgrown garden. A family with two children came to look around the property and decided that it was just what they were looking for. They would fix it up in no time. Plus, it had an amazing library that was already filled with books! The sign came down and the family moved in.

The building work began. Walls were pulled down and floors were pulled up. It was as if the house groaned. It was not long before one of the children had found an unusual book; it had a blood-red cover and its pages were completely empty – except for a charcoal smudge and a few strands of what looked like human hair. On the very first page the child wrote, 'My Stuff!' and drew a picture of herself.

Understanding the grammar and punctuation

Simple sentences

A simple sentence is made up of one main clause and a single verb.

The house was dark.

Compound sentences

A compound sentence contains two or more clauses joined by the conjunctions 'or', 'and' or 'but'.

The police searched the house from top to bottom but there was no sign of life.

Complex sentences

A complex sentence is made up of one main clause and one or more subordinate clauses.

The house was dark and, although he was afraid of being discovered, the frightened boy lit a candle.

Commas

Commas can be used to identify the different clauses in a sentence. They make the reader pause and increase the emphasis on the main clause. For example:

He felt that he had to fill up the remaining few empty leaves in his own book, that this was all that mattered.

Name

Simple, compound and complex sentences

Circle the verb in each of these simple sentences.

1. I could hear footsteps right behind me.

2. The torch fell from my clammy hand.

3. It bounced noisily down the steep steps.

4. I was left in total darkness!

5. The footsteps faded away.

6. I breathed a huge sigh of relief.

Read this passage and underline the simple sentences.

The zombie crawled out of the shallow grave and lumbered away. The children decided to follow it. Bits of dead flesh fell from its limbs but it took no notice. It smelled disgusting! Suddenly, sensing they were there, it turned and screamed at them. It was time to make a quick exit. The children fled.

Form compound sentences by joining two clauses together using one of these connectives: or, and, but or so.

1. *The eerie silence made the boy nervous _____ he started to hum a cheerful tune.*

2. *A scaly hand grabbed him from behind _____ he screamed at the top of his voice.*

3. *Blocking the door was a huge snarling dog _____ the boy had no other escape route.*

4. *A pale figure walked towards him _____ rather it floated in his direction!*

5. *The slithering noise was a venomous snake _____ I decided to leave it well alone.*

Commas

Using two different coloured pens, circle each of the two clauses that make up these sentences. The position of the commas will give you a clue!

1. *As I walked towards the old mansion, I saw a light at the window.*

2. *There was no question about it, the eyes in the picture were moving!*

3. *The last person in the line suddenly disappeared, snatched by a hungry beast.*

4. *Every muscle in his body ached, it was an effort to move.*

5. *Something was moving inside the box, so I carefully removed the lid.*

Here are some complex sentences that have commas missing. Put commas around the extra information in the sentence. Read the sentences aloud to check that they make sense.

1. *The girl who was terrified of ghosts decided not to go into the haunted house.*

2. *On the top of the hill howling at the moon was a large grey werewolf.*

3. *Looking as if he had seen a ghost the old man who lived alone quickly pulled the curtains closed.*

4. *Realising that it was her last chance to escape the girl made another grab at the rope hoping that it would hold her weight.*

5. *The castle so I have been told was once the home of an evil king who in turn was poisoned by his servant.*

Helpful hints for writing a horror story

The best horror stories are not the most gruesome tales but the ones that create suspense and fear in the mind of the reader. Here are some tips for scary writing!

✦ Bring your characters to life with vivid descriptions of their appearance and personality. Evil characters and supernatural beings often play a main role in horror stories.

✦ Horror stories are usually written in the past tense.

✦ Use dark and moody describing words to set the scene for your story. Remember to include the time and the place in which the story is set.

✦ Write your story in the third person (he, she or it).

✦ Drop hints to the reader that something strange or weird is going to happen in the story.

✦ Use pronouns to refer to any mysterious characters before telling the reader their names.

✦ Build up the tension in your story by causing characters to disappear or become trapped.

✦ Raise questions to confuse the reader. Allow them to see dangers that the characters are unaware of.

✦ Use short sentences to build up a sense of panic. Several short sentences (they may just be one or two words in length) will make the reader feel that the story is moving out of control.

✦ Include surprising events and twists in your plot. Aim to make your reader feel anxious as they meet unexpected problems.

✦ Make sure that your story includes some creepy and menacing words.

✦ Use dialogue to show what is going on in the story. You can build suspense by not saying who is speaking but rather by showing it through what is said.

✦ Most horror stories end with good overcoming evil. However, cliffhanger endings, where the reader is left to imagine the outcome, can be very effective. Decide which is best for your story.

Horror story
Scaffold 1

You are going to write a horror story.
To help plan your story, use the framework below.
Choose one option from each stage.

Stage One

Choose the characters for the story.

a) Two school friends who wanted to become famous film makers.

b) Two siblings who belonged to a nature watch group.

Stage Two

Set the scene for the story.

The children were set a project to find out about nocturnal creatures. They decided to search for them in:

a) a crumbling, disused churchyard/cemetery;

b) a derelict old mansion.

They found some tracks and decided to follow them.

Stage Three

Start your story with a good beginning.

a) The darkness seemed to suck the light out of the torch. There was just enough of a glow to see each other's terrified face and read the stark message in their eyes. 'We should go back!'

b) Hostile eyes watched the children from the shadows. This was not their place; they were intruding. They would have to pay the price.

Stage Four

Give the characters a problem.

A mysterious fog had formed and the children got lost.

a) They stumbled across a roost of giant vampire bats. In trying to escape the children became separated.

b) They realised that they were being followed by something large and angry. They started to run. One of them fell and was injured.

Stage Five

Say what happens next.

SHALL I USE THIS IDEA OR MY OWN?

a) A ghostly figure appeared and led them out of the fog to safety.

b) One child was found wandering the streets. The other had disappeared without trace.

Stage Six

Say how the story ends.

HOW SHALL I END THE STORY?

a) A story was written about their adventure and it was made into a best selling movie.

b) No one was ever told what had happened that night. The survivor never explained why their hair had turned white with fear.

Horror story
Vocabulary bank 1

anticipation	fog, mist	released
	footsteps,	
bravery	fright	scary
	frightening	scream
chase		secret, secretive
creature	ghastly, gruesome	shadow
curious	grave	shout
	groan	surprised
dark		
darkness	horrible	terror, terrifying
dashed	horror	tombstone
disappear		trapped
disbelief	moan, sigh	tremble
disused, deserted	murky	
dread		vanish
	nervous	vicious
explore		
	panic	wail
fear	pursue	warning
figure		weird, strange

My own words

Horror story
Scaffold 2

You are going to write a horror story.
To help plan your story, use the framework below.
Choose one option from each stage.

Stage One

Choose the characters and set the scene.

a) Two children, their parents and their dog who went on holiday to a castle that allowed pets to stay.

b) Two children and their dog who were sent to stay with an aunt they have never met. She was a collector of rare things.

Stage Two

Start your story with a good beginning.

a) This holiday would be one that they never forgot. It all started out so well.

b) Whining and with its tail between its legs, the dog was dragged into the hall. It did not seem to realise that this was supposed to be a pet-friendly holiday.

Stage Three

Explain what happens first in the story.

Their dog would not let them out of its sight. It growled all the time.

a) The children were allowed to go anywhere in the building. They discovered all sorts of hidden rooms and unusual items.

b) The children were allowed to go anywhere in the building except for the room on the top floor which was kept locked at all times.

They could hear faint animal cries coming from somewhere in the building.

Stage Four

Give the characters a problem.

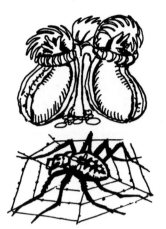

Their dog disappeared in the night. Although the children found signs of a struggle, none of the adults believed them. They realised that they would have to find their pet on their own.

a) They stole the keys to the locked rooms and came across a large rare carnivorous plant. Pets were being kept in cages to be fed to the plant. The plant would soon be large enough to produce seedlings.

b) They discovered a huge spider that had wound the dog into its web. The spider needed a host on which to lay its eggs so that its babies had something to eat. The spider would have to be destroyed.

Stage Five

Say how the problem is solved.

a) The children freed the pets/the dog which then disabled the plant/spider.

b) The aunt/owners of the castle attempted to stop the children from freeing the animals. They were grabbed by the plant/spider which gave the children and animals the chance to escape.

Stage Six

Say how the story ends.

a) A mysterious fire totally destroyed all traces of the building and its scary occupant. The holidaymakers decided to stay at home for their next vacation.

b) A pest exterminator was called in to remove the problem. It was taken to a special rare breeds zoo to be studied by scientists. Its owners were sent to jail. The holidaymakers decided to put the dog in kennels for its next holiday.

Horror story
Vocabulary bank 2

bat
bleak

capture
carnivorous
castle
cemetery
chase
chill, chilling

darkness
derelict
despair
disbelief
distress
dread
dungeon

escape
evil, vile

faint
fear, horror

gasp
ghostly
gloomy, dim
grave
graveyard

helpless
hidden, camouflaged
howl, lament

isolated

lonely, alone

nervous
nightmare
nocturnal

panic, terror

relief
rescue

secret, secretive
serpent, snake
shadowy
shiver, shake
silent, quiet
spider
swallowed

tense
torment
tower, spire
trapped, ensnared
trembling,

unusual, bizarre

vanish

wailing
warning

My own words

The birthday present

Laura looked sadly at her teddy bear. Her mum had given him to her for her last birthday and he was nearly a year old now. It was all her mum could afford since her dad had walked out. This year's birthday present wasn't going to be a pile of boxes either. Laura suddenly felt guilty. She loved her mum and she loved her teddy bear. If she was honest, they were the only real friends she had apart from Sarah. Laura told her mum some things, she told Sarah some things, but she told her teddy bear everything.

Laura gave her teddy a hug and lots of kisses and lay down on her bed cuddling him. A small tear trickled down the side of her nose. She took off her glasses and wiped her eyes. 'Ted, no one likes me you know. The boys at school said I was fat and ugly. Francesca didn't invite me to her party because she said I was too mean to buy birthday presents. I can't ask Mum for money for other people's presents, Ted. She hasn't got any money. Also, Ted, I have to keep in with the teachers in case I give Mum more worries than she's already got.' Laura was really crying now. 'And now the others are calling me "swot" and "teacher's pet". Even Sarah can't stop them calling me names. In fact, Ted,' Laura gulped, 'Sarah doesn't even try. She just laughed, when I got upset yesterday, and told me not to be so sensitive. Why is Sarah my friend, Ted? She's pretty and well off and popular, so why does she say she's my best friend?'

A tiny, nasty, squirmy little thought sneaked into Laura's head. 'Sarah's your friend because you do everything she wants because you're too scared to lose the only one who will talk to you at school,' the nasty thought whispered. Laura stuck her fingers in her ears. 'Oh, Ted,' she sighed, slipping sadly into sleep.

The next day, Laura and Sarah were in the school office, counting batches of computer tokens during lunchtime. Mrs Jones, the school secretary, told them she had to pop out to buy someone a birthday card, so they were on their own.

'Look, Laura,' Sarah said, 'Mrs Jones has left the cash box open on her desk.'

'So?' Laura asked, putting an elastic band round a hundred tokens.

'She shouldn't do that. There's loads of money in it. It's too, well, too tempting.' Sarah was gazing at the money. Laura looked at her pretty friend in surprise.

'OK. We'll tell her when she gets back. I must go to the loo. OOH, I've got cramp,' Laura said as she got up off the floor. When Laura returned from the girls' toilets, Sarah had gone. 'On my own again,' Laura thought, picking up the rest of the tokens and tidying them away.

She was thinking about the art lesson that afternoon when Mrs Jones suddenly appeared at the door and snapped, 'Laura, what are you doing?' Laura jumped, looked at her and then looked down at her hands. They were on the closed lid of the cash box.

'I'm just tidying Mrs Jones,' she said. Mrs Jones strode over and opened the cash box. It was empty.

'Where's the money, Laura?' she asked.

Laura stared at her. A horrible, sick, sinking feeling spread across her body. Tears sprung into her eyes and stuck to her lashes. 'I haven't taken it,' she wailed.

'Stop that awful noise. It was here when I left the room and now it's gone. We obviously have thieves in this school. Has anyone else been in here except you and Sarah?' Mrs Jones looked really angry.

'No,' muttered Laura.

'Have you left the office while I've been out?' Mrs Jones demanded.

'Yes, I went to the toilet,' Laura replied.

'So where have you put the money?' Mrs Jones snapped. She looked carefully at Laura and her voice softened. 'Now, come on Laura, I know things are hard for you and your Mum at home. Sarah wouldn't have taken it. Give it back to me now, before I need to tell anyone, and that will be the end of it.' Mrs Jones reached out and touched Laura's arm.

'I didn't take it, I didn't take it!' Laura could hear her voice getting louder and louder, the echoes pounding in her head. The headteacher, Miss Glinn came into the office. 'What's all the noise about?' she asked. Laura fell into a chair and began to sob.

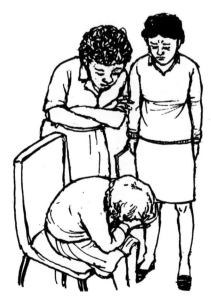

Miss Glinn, Mrs Jones, Sarah, Laura and their mums sat in the headteacher's office. Sarah, although she had taken the money, acted as if she was shocked. Her mother was outraged at being called to the school and there being even a hint that Sarah had anything to do with taking the money. 'Sarah wants for nothing Miss Glinn. Even if she were a thief – which she isn't – she wouldn't need to take anything. I resent the innuendos

that she is implicated. May I remind you that I am a governor of this school? The problem is not my daughter and if Laura was the only other person who could have taken the money, well, I shall have to leave that up to you,' Sarah's mum said. She gathered her coat and bag, 'Come along Sarah. I need to talk to you, because your choice of friends is, I think, a cause for concern. Good day Miss Glinn, Mrs Jones.' Sarah and her Mum walked out of the office.

Miss Glinn looked very, very serious. She turned to Laura's Mum. Laura's Mum bowed her head. 'Oh Laura,' she whispered.

Laura, in order to convince them, told them she knew Sarah had taken the money. No one would believe that pretty, well behaved, well off, popular Sarah would do such a thing.

'We can settle this matter easily, provided the money is returned, by keeping it to ourselves,' said Miss Glinn. Laura's mum agreed to pay back the £50 that was missing at £2.50 a week. That night as Laura lay in bed, she could hear her mum crying in the other room. 'Ted, I didn't do it,' she hissed, 'Why will no one believe me?'

Laura stood by herself in the playground, staring at her feet, before school the next morning. The other children played happily while they waited for the bell to ring. She was dreading seeing Miss Glinn and Mrs Jones. She felt sure all the other teachers would have been told she was a thief by now. She saw Sarah coming towards her. Laura scowled at her.

'Look, Laura, since you've taken the blame for the missing money, I've felt awful,' Sarah said in a low voice, 'Thanks for that, only my parents would have gone ballistic if they found out that I'd done it.'

'What about my mum?' Laura shouted.

'Ssh, Laura. I'm sorry, but everyone seemed to think that you had taken it, the way you were carrying on, and I just couldn't own up. Look, the damage has been done now. As a 'thank you' I will really look after you now. You'll see. I'll make you as popular as me. I'll tell everyone what a laugh you are, so that you get friends, and I won't let them call you names or anything,' Sarah promised.

'But why did you do it?' Laura asked.

'I spent all my allowance and I've seen some really cool trainers and, well, the money was just sitting there. Look, I really won't ever do it again. I've learned my lesson. Don't go on about it, Laura. Let's just be the very best friends. It's done now.' Sarah's face looked so pretty and she seemed so sorry that Laura said she would think about it.

The next few days were awful in one way because Laura felt the teachers were giving her funny looks and her mum was blaming herself for the trouble Laura was in. On the other hand, they were quite good because all the other children were being really nice to Laura. Sarah protected her and made her seem like the best friend in the world to have. As Laura relaxed with the other children, she found she could actually make them laugh. She learned that, unless she was easy to get on with, it was hard for others to be friendly.

Laura's birthday arrived. It was a Saturday. Laura woke up and looked at her teddy. 'It's no good, Ted. I just can't bring myself to forgive Sarah and all the stories she's told. What on earth shall I do?' she asked. Laura went down to breakfast. There was a card on the table from her Mum who had gone shopping. Laura opened the card. There was a message inside. It said:

Happy birthday, my darling. I'm so sorry but I can't give you a present this year because I have to pay the school back. If you took the money, although in my heart I don't believe you did, you can get yourself a present with that. If you didn't take the money — well, be brave and know that I will always love you.

Love Mum

Laura sat at the table and cried. There was a knock at the front door. Laura went to open it, but there was no one there, just a big, beautifully wrapped box addressed to her. Laura took it inside and opened the card that was stuck to the box. It said:

Dear Laura,

You are, first of all, the best friend ever.

I've used some of THAT money to pay you back, to say sorry and happy birthday.

Love Sarah'

Laura opened the box. Inside was a huge, silky, soft teddy bear with an enormous pink bow. Laura put on her coat, picked up the box and walked into town. She went into a charity shop.

'Yes, dear?' asked the lady behind the counter. Laura handed over the lovely teddy bear without a word and walked back home.

She went up to her room. 'Well, Ted,' she said, looking at her scruffy, little bear, 'I think the three of us have been heroes lately. It's just you and me and Mum from now onwards.' Somehow, suddenly, that thought really didn't seem so bad.

Understanding the grammar and punctuation

Plurals

A 'plural' means there is more than one of something.

Only nouns can have plurals.

Most plurals of nouns end in 's'.

(table, tables)

Here are a few other rules for plurals:

✦ If a noun ends in 'sh','ch', 's', 'ss' 'x' or 'z'

– add 'es' to make it plural.

(church, churches)

✦ If a noun ends in a consonant, followed by a 'y' change the 'y' to 'i' and add 'es.

' (story, stories)

✦ If a noun ends in a vowel followed by a 'y' add 's'.

(boy, boys)

✦ If a noun ends in with 'f' or 'fe' change the 'f' or 'fe' to 'v' and add 'es'

(thief, thieves)

Some nouns have special endings when they are made into plurals. For example:

child becomes *children*

foot becomes *feet*

Commas and adverbial phrases and clauses

An adverbial clause or phrase is a collection of words that tells us more about a verb, an adjective, another adverb or a whole sentence. They tell us these things:

How, where, when, why and what.

When the adverbial clause or phrase is written in the middle of the main clause of a sentence, it is marked off by commas. A main clause, remember, tells us the most important bit of a sentence.

So, if the main clause is *Sarah was sorry*, we could add an adverbial clause or phrase to tell us why.

Sarah, because she had taken the money, was sorry.

Name

Plurals

Rewrite these nouns in the plural.

bear _____   country _____

child _____   dish _____

teacher _____   loaf _____

man _____   speech _____

piano _____   lady _____

foot _____   half _____

glass _____   fox _____

toy _____   valley _____

Rewrite the following passage, changing the nouns to plural where appropriate. Careful – you may need to change some of the other words as well so that the sentences make sense.

The child stole the money out of the cash box and ran to the shop. In the shop was a toy mouse that had soft fur and a huge pink bow. The lady behind the counter wrapped the mouse up in a silver box and put it next to the child's foot. The child then went to the bakery. The man serving in the shop was using a knife to cut a cake in half. 'I would like a birthday cake for my friend,' said the child. 'Has she got a sweet tooth?' asked the man. 'Yes,' answered the child, 'and I am going to her party.' 'Well, have a nice day,' smiled the man.

_____

_____

_____

_____

_____

_____

_____

_____

Name

Commas

Put commas in the correct places in these sentences.

1. She just laughed when I got upset yesterday and told me not to be so sensitive.

2. Give it back to me now before I need to tell anyone and that will be the end of it.

3. Sarah although she had taken the money acted as if she was shocked.

4. I need to talk to you because your choice of friends is I think a cause for concern.

5. Laura in order to convince them told them she knew Sarah had taken the money.

6. We can settle this matter easily provided the money is returned by keeping it to ourselves.

7. Laura since you've taken the blame for the missing money I've felt awful.

Read through these sentences. The commas are in the wrong places. Rewrite each sentence showing where the commas should be.

1. Although it was pouring, with rain Tom still went fishing.

   _____

2. Providing, we have the money we will be able to go on holiday this year.

   _____

3. The man who, was very hungry couldn't, wait to buy his lunch.

   _____

4. Although injured the girl, managed to get back on her horse.

   _____

5. Sarah my, friend is very, kind.

   _____

6. Because, he was so slow Adrian always came last.

   _____

7. My, father who is extremely, tall can paint the ceiling very easily.

   _____

Helpful hints for writing a story that raises an issue

✦ An 'issue' is something that causes us problems in life. If you think about all the problems you know about, you can see that there would be plenty of issues to write about.

✦ A good place to start is to think about any problems you have had. Perhaps you have been bullied or know someone who is a bully. Perhaps you have been accused of something you didn't do, or someone thinks badly of you, which isn't fair. This would be called an 'injustice' which means 'not fair'. If you are going to write about someone dying, it may be that other people in the story don't really understand how sad your main character is.

✦ When you have decided on the issue you are going to write about, think about your feelings. Try to remember a situation you have been in or you have seen where the issue took place. How did you feel? How do you think other people around you felt?

✦ The next thing you can do is to remember exactly what happened. What led up to the situation? What happened during and after the situation? Would you have liked to change what happened during and after the situation?

✦ As you are going to write a short story, keep to a few characters. It is better to have one person who is the 'victim' and one person who is the main cause of the problem.

✦ Remember to include what people say and do. A good story will let the reader know what happens, but it will also show the reader the character's views and opinions about the events.

✦ If a character is angry, remember that they will talk in an angry way, so use words like 'shouted' and 'yelled' rather than just 'said'. An angry person will also look and move in an angry way.

✦ No-one in life is all bad or all good and your story should show this. A terrible bully may seem like the worst person in the world, but what made him/her into a bully? Try to think why they behave in this way. The victim in the story probably isn't totally 'good' either. The reader will want to be on the side of the victim, so make them human and not angels!

✦ In your writing, you can make things happen to the characters that solve the problem. If, for example, you are writing about injustice, the truth can come out or the character can accept the injustice and move on as a stronger person. Any bad people in your story can be found out, punished, made lonely, learn their lesson, be forgiven or all of these – it's up to you.

Stories that raise issues
Scaffold 1

You are going to write a story about an issue.
To help plan your story, use the framework below.
Choose one option from each stage.

Stage One

Introduce the characters and set the scene.

A boy lives with his parents. Two younger cousins come to stay
in the holidays. The cousins are twins. They are:

a) two boys;

b) two girls;

c) a boy and a girl.

Stage Two

Give the characters a plan/a change/an adventure.

The parents tell the children to go to the local shops and buy bread,
milk and a stamp for an important letter. They are to put the stamp on
the letter and post it. It is important because:

a) it is a letter from the dad accepting a new job;

b) it is a letter from the mum accepting a new job;

c) it is a letter containing the winning ticket for a prize.

Stage Three

Start the characters off on their adventure.

The children go to the shops. The boy says he will buy the bread and
milk while the twins buy the stamp and post the letter. They meet up
again to go home, but:

a) the twins have bought sweets with the stamp money;

b) the twins lost the money for the stamp;

c) the twins gave the stamp money to someone collecting money for a charity.

Without a stamp, the letter couldn't be posted, so the twins threw the letter away.

Stage Four

Give the characters a problem.

Weeks pass. The parents discover that the letter hasn't been posted because they don't get the job/prize. The twins tell the parents that:

a) they gave the letter and the stamp money to the boy;

b) they gave the stamp money to the boy who bought sweets with it;

c) they saw the boy throw the letter in a bin.

The parents are very angry with the boy. He tries to tell them the truth, but they say it is two against one.

Stage Five

Say how the problem is solved.

a) The boy has to accept that his parents will never believe him, but they will forgive him.

b) The boy is so upset, one of the twins owns up to the parents.

c) The parents hear the boy and the twins arguing. They hear the twins admitting they had not bought the stamp or posted the letter.

Stage Six

Say how the story ends.

The twins return home.

a) The parent gets a new job/wins another prize.

b) The boy decides that if anyone asks him to do something, he will do it himself and not rely on someone else.

c) The twins send the boy a parcel with an amazing present inside to say sorry.

Stories that raise issues
Vocabulary bank 1

amazing

angry · heartbroken · reprieve

anxious · · resigned

apologise · identical ·

· important · self-reliant

believe · in hot water · sticky

· irresponsible · stormed

depend upon it · ·

desolate · livid · upset

disappointed · ·

dishonest · new lease of life · vanished

· · vital

excited · owning up · waiting

fantastic · pity

frightened · pleads

furious · punishment

My own words

Stories that raise issues
Scaffold 2

You are going to write a story about an issue.
To help plan your story, use the framework below.
Choose one option from each stage.

Stage One

Introduce the characters and set the scene.

There was a boy or girl. The boy/girl is starting a new day at a new school. There is a bully in the playground who is bullying:

a) a timid girl;

b) a timid boy;

c) a small group of younger children.

Stage Two

Give the characters a plan/a change/an adventure.

In assembly, the teachers say there is going to be a crack down on:

a) rough play in the playground;

b) bullying;

c) fighting.

Stage Three

Start the characters off on their adventure.

At playtime, the new boy/girl sees the bully attacking the timid girl/boy/group of children. He/she decides to protect them and fights the bully. The bully:

a) gets a huge lump on his head;

b) gets a nose bleed;

c) gets a split lip.

The bully runs off crying to the teachers.

Stage Four

Give the characters a problem.

The new boy/girl is in big trouble with the teachers and the bully's parents. The timid boy/girl/small group of children tell the teachers it was the new boy's/girl's fault because:

a) they are still scared of the bully;

b) the bully has said he will 'get them' if they tell on him;

c) they are scared the teachers will tell them off for not reporting the bully.

WHICH PROBLEM SHALL I CHOOSE?

Stage Five

Say how the problem is solved.

a) The new boy/girl has to accept the punishment he/she is given and hopes that time will show the teachers that he/she is a good person.

b) The other children write an anonymous letter to the teachers telling them the truth.

c) There is a letter from the new girl/boy's old school saying how wonderful she/he is. The teachers realise that the new girl/boy must have had a very good reason for fighting the bully and they forgive her/him.

HOW SHALL I SOLVE THE PROBLEM?

Stage Six

Say how the story ends.

a) The bully is too afraid of the new boy/girl to bully others and he stops bullying.

b) The other children become friends with the new boy/girl and find the courage to stand up to the bully, who then stops bullying them.

c) Everyone becomes friends with the new boy/girl and the bully is very sad and lonely.

Stories that raise issues
Vocabulary bank 2

bravery	honesty	reference
charging	incidents	sent to Coventry
compassion	injustice	
consequences	insecure	temper
correspondence	intimidate	tentative
cowardly	isolation	terrorising
		threatening
distraught	melodramatic	thug
	miserable	
embarrassed		untoward
	observation	
fabrication	outrage	witness
fragile		
	punching	

My own words

The Tar Baby

Once upon a time was a merry good time
De monkey chew tabacca an' e spit white lime.
Bullfrog jump from bank ter bank
An'ain touch water till I say eh!

One sunny day, Brer Rabbie and Brer Dog were playing catch in the yard. After a while they got too hot so they sat in the shade of a coconut tree.

'Man, I's bored!' complained Brer Rabbie.

'Le's go look for some gineps in de bush,' suggested Brer Dog.

Now Brer Rabbie's mother had not given him permission to go anywhere but he was so used to doing what his friend told him, that he got right up. Brer Rabbie did not have much of a mind of his own and his mouth was watering at the thought of the sweet ginep fruits.

The two hopeful friends worked up a good sweat along the hot and dusty road. Neither of them were wearing shoes and the road tar was sticky underfoot. There was no glimpse of a ginep tree. Brer Rabbie started to grumble.

'Man, I hungry! I ain eat from lunchtime. Le's stop here an rest lil bit.'

Just then Brer Dog caught sight of something dark sitting under a nearby tree.

'Boy look ere! What dat is?' Curious, he went over to investigate. Brer Rabbie trailed behind as usual.

'What it is?' whispered Brer Rabbie in a scared voice. 'Who dis stranger is?'

Leaning against the tree trunk was a sticky black tar baby. It looked like a person but it could not speak or move. Brer Dog saw a golden opportunity to play a trick on his gullible friend. He went and stood right in front of the tar baby.

'Hey, tar baby! You look hot under dis ole tree!' Of course the tar baby said nothing.

Brer Dog told Brer Rabbie to try talking to the tar baby; perhaps it would speak to him. At once, Brer Rabbie did

what he was told. He bent down so that he was level with the tar baby's face and greeted it in a friendly manner.

'Hey frien! Wha wrong wid you?' The tar baby said nothing. Brer Rabbie tried again and again to get the tar baby to speak and each time there was no reply. Brer Dog was having a good old laugh as his friend made a fool of himself.

Now Brer Rabbie became angry at the tar baby's silence.

'Man, you's one no-manners boy, you is!' He reached out and shook the tar baby crossly.

As soon as Brer Rabbie touched the tar baby, he stuck fast. The more that he attempted to pull himself away, the more he was covered in gooey tar. He rolled around on the ground trying to get free and shouting to Brer Dog to help him.

'Brer Dog! Brer Dog! De tar baby gat me. Dis tar baby killin me!'

In the meantime, Brer Dog was laughing fit to burst, with the tears rolling down his face at his friend's plight.

'Boy! I ain never see such a ting in all my born days!'

While Brer Dog was laughing, he suddenly caught sight of a ginep tree close by. The tree was laden with fruit and he could imagine how sweet and fresh they would taste on his tongue. Without another thought for his stricken friend, he ran over and climbed the tree. Soon he had pocketfuls of the juicy fruit. He slid down the trunk and greedily began sucking the fruit's flesh from around its large stones. After a while, his stomach full, he fell asleep in the leafy shade.

Meanwhile, poor Brer Rabbie had exhausted himself with trying to escape from the sticky grasp of the silent tar baby. His entire body was coated in tar. His hair was matted and streaked with dust and his clothes were torn and tattered. He was miserable and uncomfortable and he could not believe that Brer Dog had gone off and left him.

Some time later Brer Dog woke up feeling much refreshed. He decided that he would need help to free his friend from the tar baby and set off back to the village. On the way he met Brer Crab, who immediately agreed to come and rescue poor Brer Rabbie.

The only way to free Brer Rabbie and clean him off was to rub him hard with kerosene soaked rags. The kerosene was very smelly and it stung his skin. It took Brer Dog and Brer Crab a long time to make him look presentable. Brer Rabbie was furious with Brer Dog for the trick he had played on him. He kept shouting, 'You is ter blame! You cause de whole ting.'

'I ain do nuttin!' replied Brer Dog. 'You is too fool if you try to talk to one tar baby!' and with that he ran off as fast as he could. Well child, that Brer Dog ran that quick that there was no way that Brer Rabbie could catch him. He looked everywhere, all the time cursing his wicked friend.

Brer Crab shook his head at all Brer Rabbie's complaining.

'Man, you know dat Brer Dog is one tricky fellow,' he remarked wisely, 'Why you go an' do as he say? You mus think afor you act!' With that he left Brer Rabbie to make his own way home. Boy, was there trouble when his Ma saw the state of his clothes and his skin! She tanned his tail with her slipper and gave him a whole heap of chores to do.

Now, Brer Rabbie was a kind-hearted chap, if a little easily led and it wasn't long before he missed Brer Dog's company. He decided that his friendship was worth more than the mean trick that had been played upon him. I am sure that Brer Dog would agree – once he comes out of hiding!

E-bo ben'
My ole story en'
I'll never tell a big lie
Like dat again!

The moral of this story is that you ought to think about the consequences of your actions and not blindly follow what others tell you.

Understanding the grammar and punctuation

Identifying word classes

Some words can be changed in particular ways. Recognising the endings can help you to identify different word classes.

Verb endings change when the tense of the verb is altered.

He looks (present)

He will look (future)

He looked (past)

Nouns change when you make them plural.

Coconut – coconuts
baby – babies

Using adjectives to compare things changes their endings.

sticky – stickier – stickiest

Using local dialects in your writing

People change the way that they speak depending on where they are and what they are doing. In a formal situation they will speak in standard English but, when out with their friends, they may speak in their local dialect, using different words and phrases.

'Boy look ere, I reach!'

is Bahamian dialect for

'Hello, I have arrived!'

Writing conversations in dialect can make your story characters more realistic.

Using speech marks

Speech marks (' ') are used to show direct speech. There are three types of direct speech:

Type 1: The speech goes at the beginning of the sentence. For example:

'Man, I's bored!' complained Brer Rabbie.

Type 2: The speech goes at the end of the sentence. For example:

He kept shouting, 'You is ter blame!'

Type 3: The sentence of speech is split, coming at the beginning and end of the main sentence For example:

'Man, you know dat Brer Dog is one tricky fellow,' he remarked wisely, 'Why you go an' do as he say? You mus think afor you act!'

Name

Word classes

Read the following story about a Bahamian flamingo. See how many different word classes you can find. Write each word in the correct box.

Once there was a flamingo whose feathers were more beautiful than those of any of his friends. They were the deepest shade of pink that had ever been seen. This flamingo became very vain and decided that since he was the most handsome of all the flamingos, he ought to eat special food.

'You dull, dull birds wid your pale pink feathers, you's can eat all dese lil shrimp. I will eat only dose bright silver fish!'

Well, child, from that time he only ate shiny silver fish; while his friends swallowed tiny shrimps.

Then one day the conceited flamingo noticed that his friends were laughing at him from behind their wings. He looked at his reflection in the lagoon and saw that his feathers were a dull grey colour. All his bright pink colours had faded away! He was so embarrassed that he flew to another island to hide.

He did not realise that it is the humble pink shrimp that gives the colour to a flamingo's feathers!

Nouns	Adjectives	Verbs	Adverbs

What is the moral of this story? _____

Read the following morals. On the back of this sheet, write in your own words what each one means. Share your ideas with a friend.

A stitch in time saves nine.

If you can't stand the heat get out of the kitchen.

Name

Using speech marks

Punctuate the following three types of speech using speech marks.

1. *Man it hot today! gasped Brer Rabbie.*

2. *Brer Crab nodded, That is for sure.*

3. *I know, exclaimed Brer Rabbie, let's go swimming in the sea.*

4. *I'll race you to the water, shouted Brer Crab, last one in is a fool.*

5. *Oh good, here comes my dinner, grinned Brer Shark!*

Rewrite this conversation in standard English and punctuate it using speech marks.

1. *Where you is? What you doing? called my Mother.*

    _____

2. *I's right here, I replied. I ain't do nothing!*

    _____

3. *Ain't you got no homework? she asked.*

    _____

4. *I done my spelling and I ain't got no maths.*

    _____

5. *It were lucky I asked, she grinned. I needs help with these dirty dishes!*

    _____

    _____

Make up a conversation between two of your own characters.
Include some dialect phrases.

Helpful hints for writing a traditional tale from the Bahamas

✦ Give your story a tropical island setting. Describe the golden sandy beaches, the clear blue water and the hot sunny weather.

✦ Traditional tales all start with the same beginning:

Once upon a time was a merry good time
De monkey chew tabacca an' e spit white lime.
Bullfrog jump from bank ter bank
An'ain touch water till I say eh!

They all finish with the same ending:

E-bo ben'
My ole story en'
I'll never tell a big lie
Like dat again!

✦ Most Bahamian stories are written in the third person.

✦ Try using one of these everyday settings in your story: the beach, the market, sailing or fishing in a boat, looking after animals like goats and pigs, going to school and finding shady places to keep out of the sun.

✦ Old Bahamian houses were usually made from wood and had a veranda where people would sit and chat. They were often painted in bright colours and had banana and coconut trees planted close by.

✦ If you are writing a Brer Rabbit style story, remember to give your animal characters human characteristics. They might be selfish, lazy, greedy or kind.

✦ In your story, mention Bahamian things like the plants and the foods. Use the vocabulary bank to give you ideas.

✦ A lot of Bahamian stories are about children who get up to mischief and learn things the hard way.

✦ Choose Bahamian names for the people in your story. Look for examples in Vocabulary bank 2.

✦ When you are writing dialogue, try to include some local dialect phrases. The vocabulary bank can help you with this.

✦ Other recurring characters in Bahamian stories are the Jumbey (ghost) and the Bugga man (he eats bad children).

✦ Your story should contain a moral.

Traditional tales from the Bahamas
Scaffold 1

You are going to write a traditional Brer Rabbie style Bahamian tale.
To help you plan your story, use the framework below.
Choose one option from each stage.

Stage One

Choose the characters for your story.

Brer Rabbie and any one of the following: Brer Crab, Brer Goat,
Brer Dog, Brer Flamingo or Brer Parrot.

Stage Two

Start your story with a good beginning.

Once upon a time was a merry good time
De monkey chew tabacca an' e spit white lime.
Bullfrog jump from bank ter bank
An'ain touch water till I say eh!

a) Once there were two friends who lived on a beautiful island.
   One of them was hard working and the other was very lazy.

b) Once there were two friends who lived in a wooden house on the beach. One of them was
   kind but the other was selfish.

Stage Three

Set the scene for the story.

The friends decided to have a beachcombing competition to see
who could find the most unusual item.

a) They set off in the same direction and raced over to any
   strange shape that they spotted on the sand.

b) One friend decided to follow the other to spy on what they
   find.

Stage Four

Give the characters a problem.

Suddenly they came to a large rock pool. There was something thrashing about in the shallow water.

a) It was an injured turtle that could not climb out to get back to the sea.

b) It was a fish that hardly had enough water to swim around in.

The poor creature begged the friends for help.

Stage Five

Say how the problem is solved.

a) Without a second thought, the kind character immediately started to assist the creature back into the sea. The selfish character decided that they could not spare the time because they wanted to win the competition.

c) The hardworking character struggled to carry the creature back to the sea. The lazy character thought it was too much trouble to bother with and carried on beachcombing.

The rescued creature rewarded the character with a knobbly grey shell and told them not to look inside until the end of the competition.

Stage Six

Say how the story ends.

The two beachcombers brought their finds back to the house. One had the dull shell and the other had found a wooden casket that tinkled when you shook it. On the count of three they opened them up.

a) Inside the shell was a beautiful luminous pearl. Inside the casket were a few rusty old fishhooks.

b) Inside the shell was a golden coin from a sunken galleon. Inside the casket were a couple of old spoons.

I think that you can judge for yourself who the winner was!

E-bo ben'
My ole story en'
I'll never tell a big lie
Like dat again!

The moral of this story is:

a) One good turn deserves another.

b) Appearances are deceptive.

Traditional tales from the Bahamas
Vocabulary bank 1

animals
bird
chicken
crab
dog
dolphin
fish
flamingo
goat
iguana
mosquito
parrot
pig
shark
turtle

fruits
banana
coconut
gineps
mango
plantain

farming
collect eggs
dig
feed hens
harvest
look after goats/pigs
plant
pull up weeds
sow seeds

fishing
bait
boat
cast
net
haul
hook
row

places
sandy beach
coral
reef
market place
field
village
yard

My own words

Traditional tales from the Bahamas
Scaffold 2

You are going to write a Bahamian traditional tale.
To help plan your story, use the framework below.
Choose one option from each stage.

Stage One

Choose the characters for your story.

Once upon a time was a merry good time
De monkey chew tabacca an' e spit white lime.
Bullfrog jump from bank ter bank
An'ain touch water till I say eh!

In a brightly painted wooden house on a beautiful tropical island there lived:

a) two mischievous siblings and their elderly grandmother;

b) two cousins and their uncle.

Stage Two

Start your story with a good beginning.

a) The children crept silently past the snoozing figure on the porch. It was the creaking of the last wooden step that gave them away; 'Exactly where do you two think you are going?'

b) 'The Bugga will come looking for you wid he sack and eat up your bones, if you ain't fix up those nails!' The children glumly picked up their hammers.

Stage Three

Set the scene for the story.

The children had been told to hammer down any nails that had come loose around the house and the fences. The sun was very hot and they did not think that the job they had been given was important. Instead they slipped off to the beach.

a) They went fishing and then sold their catch at the market. They spent all the money on themselves.

b) They swam out to the reef and spent their time swimming with the turtles and dolphins. When a shark came to investigate what was going on, the children hurried back to the shore!

Stage Four

Give the characters a problem.

Later that day a tropical storm hit the island. The strong winds and rain caused a lot of damage. Wherever a nail was loose the planks were ripped off.

a) The animals escaped through the broken fence; they destroyed the family's crops and then ran away.

b) The wind blew the unfastened planks off the roof and the downpour drenched many of the rooms.

Stage Five

Say how the problem is solved.

The children did not want to get into trouble, so they did not mention that they failed to mend the loose nails. That night they heard the Bugga man trying to get in through their window. He wanted to put them in his sack.

a) The family dog barked and warned off the Bugga man.

b) The noise woke up their grandmother/uncle and the Bugga man disappeared.

Stage Six

Say how the story ends.

a) The children owned up and worked very hard to help sort out the mess they had caused. They had no time to go to the beach.

b) The children had to do lots of jobs to earn enough money to replace all the lost planks. Any time they felt like shirking they remember the Bugga man.

E-bo ben'
My ole story en'
I'll never tell a big lie
Like dat again!

The moral of this story is:

a) A stitch in time saves nine.   b) Prevention is better than a cure.

Traditional tales from the Bahamas
Vocabulary bank 2

people

cousin

father

farmer

fisherman

friend

grandmother

market seller

mother

old man

old woman

plants

hibiscus

palm trees

jasmine

frangipani

scary characters

bugga man

jumbey (ghost)

vegetables

avocado

carrots

corn

onions

sweet potatoes

peppers

weather

damp

heat

hot

humid

hurricane

rain

sun

sunny

sweltering

thunder

torrential

tropical

warm

dialect phrases

What it is? – What is it?

Where you is? – Where
   are you?

I reach – I am here

I ain for that – I don't
   want to

Boy look ere! – Hey!

I ain do nuttin! – I didn't
   do it!

I tired – I am tired

I hungry – I am hungry

Bahamian female names

Latoya

Keisha

Paulette

Samaria

Shakera

Shanette

Stevenette

Tamika

Waynette

Bahamian male names

Curtis

Deangelo

Deanza

Deshawn

Desmond

Godfrey

Lavardo

Tameko

My own words

The Fisher-of-the Land

A long time ago after the creation of the world, the demigod Maui lived in Hawaiki. Rather than going out fishing with his brothers, he would lounge around, listening to the gossip of the women in the village. His female relatives would chide him for his laziness and at last Maui could stand their taunts no longer.

The next time that his brothers were getting ready to go on a fishing trip, Maui asked if he could accompany them.

'No, you will only cause trouble!' they cried and left him standing on the shore.

Maui was not to be easily discouraged. Instead, he watched for his brothers' return and – under the cover of darkness – when certain that his actions would go unnoticed, he hid himself beneath the decking of the canoe.

The following day, he waited until they had paddled a fair distance from the beach – then he emerged from his cramped hiding place. His brothers were furious and started to turn the canoe around to put him ashore. However, Maui used his magical powers to make the coast appear further away than it really was; so his brothers decided that it would be easier to let him stay aboard (he even offered to bail the water from the canoe.)

The brothers paddled on to their normal fishing grounds but Maui insisted that they should go out to the open sea and fish there.

'If you go to the place that I choose, I promise that you will catch many more fish and we can return home more quickly.'

The brothers were unsure about this but at last, after much discussion, they agreed. So they paddled still further and soon the land was lost from view.

'This a good spot!' exclaimed Maui finally. 'Cast your hooks over the side here!'

The brothers did as he told them and no sooner had the hooks sunk beneath the surface of the deep blue water than ... the fish started to bite.

Shouting with glee, the brothers hauled them into the canoe and in no time at all it was full of flapping, silver fish. The brothers decided that they should head back to the village with their amazing catch. They were making ready for the return trip when Maui cried out:

'Let me try my fish hook!'

This magic hook had been carved from the jawbone of one of his ancestors, who had been a sorcerer. It was a beautifully decorated lure; carved with great imagination and skill; shining with the iridescent hues of paua shell and sporting hair from a white dog's tail.

'Let me have some bait,' urged Maui, but his brothers refused. Undeterred, Maui smeared his own blood on the hook; tying it to a strong rope, he dropped it over the side of the canoe.

All at once there was a huge jerk and the line went taut: Maui could tell that an immense fish had taken his hook.

Despite the wild struggling of the great fish, Maui slowly drew it up from the depths of the sea. His brothers feared for their lives as the canoe was tossed like a twig on the mercilessly thrashing waves.

'We will be drowned!' they wailed in despair.

Maui ignored their cries. Chanting incantations, he focused all his attention on dragging in the massive catch. At last a huge land-fish (land in the shape of a fish) appeared at the surface and, as Maui continued to wind in the rope, the canoe was left high and dry on the land that he had pulled from the sea. So it was that Maui became the Fisher-of-the-Land.

Note:
The land that Maui pulled up was in the shape of a fish. This 'fish' became the North Island of New Zealand, referred to by the ancient Maori as 'the fish of Maui' or Te ika a Maui ('te ika' means 'the fish').

The South Island became known as 'the canoe of Maui' or Te waka a Maui ('te waka' means 'the canoe'), in which he was sitting when he caught the great land-fish.

Stewart Island, just to the south of the South Island was called 'the anchor of Maui' or Te punga a Maui ('te punga' means 'the anchor').

Understanding the grammar and punctuation

Commas

Commas are used to separate parts of a sentence. They tell the reader when to take a pause.

The following day, he waited...

However, Maui used his magical powers...

Semi-colons

A semi-colon looks like this ;
It is used to divide clauses in a sentence or to separate complicated items in a list.

Undeterred, Maui smeared his own blood on the hook; tying it to a strong rope, he dropped it over the side of the canoe.

Brackets, commas and dashes

Brackets, commas and dashes can all be used to separate an extra piece of information from the main part of the sentence.

The following day he waited until they had paddled a fair distance from the beach – then he emerged from his cramped hiding place.

So his brothers decided that it would be easier to let him stay aboard, (he even offered to bail the water from the canoe).

The brothers were unsure about this but at last, after much discussion, they agreed.

Colons

A colon looks like this :
It is used to introduce lists, speech, an idea or an explanation in a sentence.

All at once there was a huge jerk and the line went taut: Maui could tell that an immense fish had taken his hook.
Maui cried out: 'Let me try my fish hook.'

Connectives

A connective is a word or phrase that links clauses or sentences.

'Let me have some bait,' urged Maui <u>but</u> his brothers refused.

Connectives include:

next, because, later, and, but, when, therefore, however, consequently

Connectives

Choose connectives from the box below to complete these sentences.

but	if	and	so	because	or

1. I can only go out in the boat _____ you come too.

2. He wants to try his hand at fishing _____ he does not have a rod.

3. The women thought Maui was lazy _____ he lay around in the sun all day.

4. Would you like to sit at the front of the boat _____ the back?

5. The storm caused huge waves _____ I was very afraid.

6. The fish was dying out of the water _____ he decided to return it to the sea.

7. You may hold my fishing rod _____ you promise not to break it.

8. There is a storm coming _____ we will have to head back to the harbour.

9. She was proud _____ he had caught the biggest fish of the day.

10. I caught a shark _____ I have the photograph to prove it!

Read this passage and underline all the connectives that you can find.

Suddenly, Maui was discovered in the boat. His brothers could not decide whether to throw him overboard or allow him to stay. The brothers were annoyed because they had not caught any fish. Moreover, they were tired of Maui's tricks so they wanted to teach him a lesson. Finally, they agreed to let him fish so long as he gave them his catch. Within moments the nets were full with fish and everyone was happy.

Use two of the connectives in a sentence of your own.

Commas, dashes and brackets

Rewrite these sentences, putting commas, dashes or brackets in them.

1. *Maui a lazy trickster hid in the bow of the boat.*

   _____

2. *I caught a fish but it got away honestly!*

   _____

3. *Maui pulled the dry land out of the ocean it was rather heavy.*

   _____

4. *The fisherman happy with his catch headed back to shore.*

   _____

5. *The bait a worm wriggled on the palm of my hand.*

   _____

Semicolons (;)

Put a semicolon into the correct place in each sentence.

1. *Rata looked all through the forest for the straightest tree only the best would do for his canoe.*

2. *As night fell the kiwi emerged pushing aside leaves it searched for insects with its long beak.*

3. *Tane Mahuta was the God of the Forest he looked after all the trees and wildlife.*

Colon (:)

Put a colon into the correct place in each sentence.

1. *On this shark fishing trip you will need a strong rod, live bait, sharp hooks and a lot of luck!*

2. *The boat was sinking fast the water was icy cold and very wet.*

3. *Once the tree was felled the real work began the branches were cut off, the bark removed and the shape of a canoe chiselled out of the trunk.*

Helpful hints for writing a Maori legend

✦ Your story should be set in the past.

✦ Most myths are told using a third person narrator.

✦ Maori stories were not written down, they were passed on from person to person through story telling. Key characters would stay the same but descriptions would differ.

✦ Maori myths and legends are concerned with the creation of the world, explaining the features of the natural world and telling stories about heroes and heroines.

✦ Many Maori legends tell of the actions of the demi-god, Maui. He is usually portrayed as a bit of a trickster but very brave.

✦ The plot of many of these stories is about the hero completing a special task or defeating a monster.

✦ The sea and sea monsters are key elements of many of these old stories. The people who first came to New Zealand used boats a lot to get about and go fishing. Think of some interesting similes to describe the ocean and its creatures.

✦ One of the most common monsters is the taniwha (pronounced 'tan-i-fa-which). People could ask them for help but they also had to make sure that they did not displease them in any way.

✦ Your main character might have magical powers or a magical item such as the fishing hook in *The Fisher-of-the-Land* story.

✦ Your story does not have to have a happy ending.

Maori legend
Scaffold 1

You are going to write a Maori legend.
To help plan your story, use the framework below.
Choose one option from each stage.

Stage One

Choose the character for your story.

a) Tane-Mahuta, god of nature and of trees.

b) Rata, a hero who wanted to return his dead father's body
to his home.

Stage Two

Start your story with a good beginning.

Wandering sadly amongst the mighty trees of the forest, he stared
intently at the trees rising high above his head, at the width of
the trunks, the strength of the branches.

a) He noticed that they were starting to sicken because bugs were eating
them.

b) He needed to make a waka (canoe) and the totara tree seemed to be
the most suitable tree for the task. He set about cutting down the tree.

Stage Three

Set the scene for the story

a) Tane-Mahuta talked to his brother, Tane-Hokahoka, who called all of the birds of the air
together. Tane-Mahuta explained that he needed one of the birds to come down and live
on the forest floor; there they would eat the bugs that were killing the trees.

b) The next day when Rata returned to where he had cut down the tree, he found that it was
standing tall again. Once again he chopped it down and hollowed out the trunk. On the
following day the tree was standing untouched as before. He cut it down yet again and
watched to see what happened.

Stage Four

Give the characters a problem.

a) The Tui was too scared of the dark to come down. The Pukeko did not want to get his feet wet on the damp ground and the Pipiwharauroa was too busy building his nest. Every bird came up with an excuse as to why they could not leave the tree tops.

b) Every night the birds and insects would rebuild the tree and make it whole again. Rata would not be able to build the canoe to fetch his father's body. Rata heard strange singing and realised that it was the god of the trees.

Stage Five

Say how the problem is solved.

Tane-Mahuta, god of the trees explained that:

a) If no bird offered to eat the bugs on the forest floor then the trees would die. The kiwi did not wish to leave the sunny tree tops but it decided that it would help the trees; even if this meant losing its lovely coloured feathers and its wings.

b) Rata had not asked permission to use the tree. Rata was very sorry for what he had done and promised not to cut down any trees again without the tree god's permission.

Stage Six

Say how the story ends.

Tane-Mahuta was very pleased with this decision. As a reward,

a) the kiwi was made the most well known and most loved bird of them all.

b) he gave Rata a mighty war canoe.

Maori legend
Vocabulary bank 1

afraid, fearful
ask, request
axe – toki
birds
branch, bough
carved
confused
coward
dawn
decided
father
forest
forgive
gloomy, shady
hacked, cut
insects
leaves, twigs
lush

morning, daybreak
permission
promise
puzzled
Rata – legendary hero
reward
sick, diseased
straight, upright
suitable
sunlight
think, consider
totara tree
towering
trunk, log
waka – canoe
wandering

<u>Maori gods</u>
Tane-Hokahoka – god
 of birds
Tane-Mahuta – god of
 trees

<u>New Zealand birds</u>
kiwi – flightless bird
 that eats insects
pipiwharauroa – lays
 its eggs in other
 birds' nests
pukeko – lives in
 swampy areas
tui – songbird with
 white feathers at its
 throat

My own words

Maori legend
Scaffold 2

You are going to write a Maori legend.
To help plan your story, use the framework below.
Choose one option from each stage.

Stage One

Choose the characters for your story.

a) a taniwha (a mythical dragon).

b) a tribe.

Stage Two

Start your story with a good beginning.

Once in Aotearoa, the Land of the Long White Cloud there was a taniwha that lived peacefully in a forest stronghold, in a great range of mountains / a tribe that lived in a large, prosperous village at the mouth of a harbour.

a) The taniwha was often hungry. His favourite place to find food was from a settlement by a harbour, where the people got plump on all the seafood they caught.

b) Yet another great war canoe could be seen on the horizon. It was heading their way! The look-out raised the alarm.

Stage Three

Set the scene for the story.

a) Outside the calm waters of the harbour lurked a giant octopus. It had huge snaking tentacles and preyed on unsuspecting fishermen.

b) The entrance to the harbour was so sheltered that invading war tribes could easily land their waka and wreak havoc in the village: fighting their warriors and stealing the crops. They realised that they needed to improve their defences.

Stage Four

Give the characters a problem.

a) A rock slide widened the entrance to the harbour and the octopus was able to attack the people in the village. The taniwha was angry with the intruder and bit off one of his tentacles. The octopus returned to the sea to plan its revenge.

b) Two taniwha (sea dragons) were put in place to guard the entrance to the harbour. One of these great monsters made its home at the south head and the other at the north.

Stage Five

Say how the problem is solved.
Each of these mighty creatures had its task to perform.

a) The octopus built a staircase of rock to reach the taniwha and they had a great fight. The octopus managed to drown the taniwha and throw his body into the mountains: before he himself died of his injuries.

b) The taniwha had huge, powerful tails and they used these to churn up the ocean water, so that the attacking waka would be swamped by the waves and sink.

Stage Six

Say how the story ends.

From that time the people in the village felt a lot safer because:

a) The body of the octopus was dragged back to the ocean depths by its family. The taniwha's body slowly turned to stone and was transformed into a mighty mountain.

b) The entrance to the harbour could only be navigated by those waka that posed no threat to the tribe.

Maori Legend
Vocabulary bank 2

Aotearoa – Maori name for New Zealand meaning: Land of the Long White Cloud

alarm

attack, raid

battle

bold, fearless

bravery

combat

creature

entrance, head

forest

frightening, scary

guard

harbour

hauled, dragged

havoc

helpless

horizon, distance

invader

lash out

lived in fear

monster

mountain range

mysterious

mystical

ocean

octopus

plunder

raise the alarm

rocks, boulders, stones

safe, secure

safe haven

settlement, village

strength

swamped, flooded

tail

taniwha – legendary dragon that lives in deep pools and dark caves

tentacle

tribe

waka – canoe

warrior

waves, swell

wounded, injured

My own words